COUNTRIES OF THE WORLD

Scotland

Gareth Stevens Publishing
A WORLD ALMANAC EDUCATION GROUP COMPANY

About the Author: Lise Hull is a freelance writer and researcher whose heritage is partly Scottish. She has traveled extensively throughout Great Britain, is passionate about British castles, and enjoys attending Highland Games and clan gatherings.

Written by
LISE HULL

Edited by
KATHARINE BROWN

Edited in U.S. by
PATRICIA LANTIER
MONICA RAUSCH

Designed by
SANDY SUM

Picture research by
SUSAN JANE MANUEL

First published in North America in 2001 by
Gareth Stevens Publishing
A World Almanac Education Group Company
330 West Olive Street, Suite 100
Milwaukee, Wisconsin 53212 USA

Please visit our web site at:
www.garethstevens.com
For a free color catalog describing
Gareth Stevens' list of high-quality books
and multimedia programs, call
1-800-542-2595 (USA) or
1-800-461-9120 (CANADA).
Gareth Stevens Publishing's
Fax: (414) 332-3567.

© **TIMES MEDIA PRIVATE LIMITED 2001**
Originated and designed by
Times Editions
An imprint of Times Media Private Limited
A member of the Times Publishing Group
Times Centre, 1 New Industrial Road
Singapore 536196
http://www.timesone.com.sg/te

Library of Congress Cataloging-in-Publication Data
Hull, Lise.
Scotland / by Lise Hull.
p. cm. — (Countries of the world)
Includes bibliographical references and index.
ISBN 0-8368-2339-7 (lib. bdg.)
1. Scotland — Juvenile literature. [1. Scotland.] I. Title.
II. Countries of the world (Milwaukee, Wis.)
DA762.H85   2001
941.1—dc21   2001017029

Printed in Malaysia

1 2 3 4 5 6 7 8 9 05 04 03 02 01

Contents

AN OVERVIEW OF SCOTLAND

Often associated with bagpipes and kilts, Scotland is a fascinating country, with friendly, outgoing people. From ancient standing stones to medieval castles, Scottish history can be traced through its romantic ruins and intriguing traditions. The mountains of the north contrast with the farmlands and industrial centers of central and southern Scotland, as do the lifestyles of people living in each area. Scots are passionately devoted to their homeland and have fought for centuries to remain an independent nation. Although Scotland today is a part of the United Kingdom of Great Britain and Northern Ireland, along with England, Wales, and Northern Ireland, the country is partially independent with its own parliament, education system, and religion.

Opposite: **Street performers entertain a crowd of shoppers on the Royal Mile in Edinburgh, Scotland's capital city.**

Below: **Young boys wearing traditional Scottish dress take a break during the 1998 World Pipe Championship in Glasgow and have fun on a bouncy castle.**

THE FLAG OF SCOTLAND

Scotland's official flag is the cross of Saint Andrew, also known as the Saltire. The white, x-shaped cross is set against an azure-blue background and honors Saint Andrew, the patron saint of Scotland. Legend has it that before the Picts and Scots fought the Anglo-Saxon Northumbrians in the ninth or tenth century, a group of white clouds shaped like Saint Andrew's cross appeared in the blue sky. The Picts and Scots believed these clouds predicted their victory. The following day, the Picts and Scots defeated the Northumbrians. The flag came into widespread use in the fifteenth century.

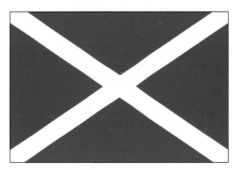

Geography

Scotland lies immediately north of England and occupies about one-third of the island of Great Britain. Water borders Scotland on three sides: the Atlantic Ocean pounds the coastline to the north and west, and the North Sea lies to the east. Of Scotland's 787 islands, 130 are inhabited. Situated off the western coast are the Hebrides, the largest group in Scotland with nearly five hundred islands. The Outer Hebrides, also called the Western Isles, include, among others, Lewis, North Uist, and South Uist. The Inner Hebrides include Jura, Skye, Iona, and Mull. The Orkney Islands are off the northeastern coast, and the Shetland Islands are located northeast of the Orkney Islands. Scotland has an area of 30,418 square miles (78,783 square kilometers), including inhabited islands.

From north to south, Scotland can be divided into three geographical areas: the Highlands, the Central Lowlands, and the Southern Uplands. Dominated by mountains and dramatic scenery, the Highlands make up more than half of Scotland's landmass. A geological fault line known as the Great Glen divides the Highlands into two regions. Along the Great Glen lie many of Scotland's lochs, or lakes, including Loch Ness.

LOCH NESS AND ITS MONSTER

Over 750 feet (229 meters) deep and 23 miles (37 km) long, Scotland's Loch Ness is believed by many to be home to an unidentified aquatic creature affectionately named "Nessie."
(A Closer Look, page 54)

Below: Lush fields and breathtaking views are a common sight in the Central Lowlands.

Southeast of the Great Glen are the Grampian Mountains. The highest peak in the Grampians and Britain's highest summit is Ben Nevis at 4,406 feet (1,343 meters). The Grampians surround an enormous flat area of bogs and deep lochs, known as the Moor of Rannoch. At the southern end of the Great Glen is Loch Lomond, which, at 27 square miles (70 square km), is Scotland's largest stretch of inland water.

South of the Highlands are the Central Lowlands, a narrow belt of land that covers about one-tenth of the area of Scotland. This region is flatter, lusher, and less rugged than the Highlands. Scotland's largest cities — Edinburgh, the country's capital, and Glasgow — are located here. This area is also home to rich farmlands, most of the nation's industries, and a majority of the country's population.

The Southern Uplands are not as high in elevation as the Highlands and include the Scottish Borders, an area of land close to England, and hilly countryside. The Cheviot Hills form the border with England.

Scotland is characterized by many streams, lochs, and rivers. The longest river in Scotland is the Tay, which runs about 120 miles (193 km). It is also one of Europe's richest salmon rivers. Other main rivers include the Clyde, Dee, Forth, Spey, and Tweed.

Above: **The city of Perth is located on the banks of the River Tay. For centuries, Perth has been a trading center for leather products and wool. The city has become a major link between the Highland and Lowland regions.**

THE CAIRNGORMS

Situated southeast of the Great Glen are the Cairngorm Mountains, a range of mountains that rises from a giant plateau. One hundred and six peaks in the range are over 3,000 feet (914 m).

Climate

Although Scotland is close to the Arctic Circle, wind from the southwest blows over a continuation of the warm Gulf Stream in the North Atlantic. This wind has a moderating effect on the country's climate. The western islands and coastline tend to be wetter and warmer than eastern Scotland, which frequently suffers from brisk winds blowing from the North Sea. The Highlands and northern islands generally have the harshest weather. Winter temperatures in Scotland average between 37° Fahrenheit (2.8° Celsius) and 41° F (5° C). Scottish summers are also cool, as temperatures only reach an average of 59° F (15° C). While annual rainfall averages 32.5 inches (82.5 centimeters) throughout Scotland, western Scotland sometimes has over 115 inches (292 cm) in one year.

Plant and Animal Life

Scotland's plants and animals vary greatly from region to region. Squat plants accustomed to colder climates, such as mosses, grow well in the northern mountains and hills. The lowlands and moors of central and southern Scotland are covered with lush grasses and purple heather, and boggy areas are rich in peat. Scotland is sparsely forested, most commonly with conifers and oak trees.

THE ANCIENT ORKNEYS

Affected by westerly winds and gales, the Orkney Islands are home to numerous historical sites that provide invaluable insight into late Neolithic life.
(A Closer Look, page 44)

Below: **Eilean Donan Castle is covered with snow during the cold winter months. Located near Dornie, the castle was built in about 1260. The castle lay in ruins for almost two hundred years before being restored in 1912 and is now the seat of the Clan MacRae.**

Left: **A puffin sits on the edge of a cliff along the western coast of the Highlands. It nests on seaside and island cliffs and can be recognized by its large, brightly colored, triangular beak.**

Scotland's animals have adapted to the variations in local geography. Although many native species have died out, two that still freely wander the Scottish Highlands are Shetland ponies and Highland cattle. The small size and thick coats of the ponies have allowed them to survive the harsh winters, as have the shaggy coats and long horns of the cattle. Mountain hares, pine martens, wildcats, and endangered red squirrels occupy the wooded areas of the Highlands. Herds of red deer, Britain's largest wild animal, also live in the Highlands. Other common animal species include field mice, voles, shrews, badgers, foxes, hedgehogs, and minks.

About half of the world's gray seals breed in Scottish waters, particularly around the northern and western islands. Dolphins and porpoises often appear here, and whales occasionally can be spotted, especially on the western coast. Otters live along the coasts and in sea lochs.

Majestic birds, such as golden eagles, buzzards, and kestrels, fly throughout the mountainous areas, while ospreys hunt for fish near freshwater or sea lochs. At lower elevations, grouse, greyling geese, kittiwakes, puffins, and various types of gulls make themselves at home.

SCOTLAND'S WILDFLOWERS

Wildflower species color the countryside and include wood anemones, cowslips, wild hyacinths, red campions, primroses, mistletoe, orchids, and alpine lady's mantles. Whether in the woods, the Lowlands, the mountains, or even in the boggy areas, Scottish wildflowers add great beauty to the scenery.

History

Human settlement in Scotland began in the third millennium B.C. By the second millennium B.C., Neolithic farmers began to occupy the northernmost regions of Scotland. They lived in settlements and grew crops.

In about 1800 B.C, during the Bronze Age, a new group of people entered Scotland. Called the "Beaker folk" because of the shape of their drinking vessels, these people lived in northern Scotland and erected hundreds of standing stones and circles. Other European peoples arrived in Scotland in the first millennium B.C. They brought iron implements and constructed heavier fortifications. The Romans conquered England in A.D. 43, but they did not extend their rule over the land they called Caledonia, due to strong resistance from the Picts and the other European groups.

In the first century, Britons from the south began to move into Scotland, while Scots from Ireland and Angles from northern Europe came in the fifth century. These three groups gradually merged with the Picts and earlier European groups to form a single nation, thereafter known as Scotland, in the eleventh century.

Above: The Picts, also known as the painted people, were ancient inhabitants of northern and central Scotland. They were the most powerful tribal group in Scotland, and members intimidated their enemies by painting and tattooing their bodies. They lived in defended settlements, or hill forts.

Feudalism

In the twelfth century, Scotland's King David I (r. 1124–1153) encouraged Anglo-Norman families to settle in Scotland. With their arrival, the feudal system of government was established. This system reinforced the authority of the king and divided the country's lands among loyal subjects. These subjects, in turn, provided men for the king's army and demanded high rent from the Scots working in their fields.

Traditionally, Scottish society had been based on tribal relationships. Members were associated by blood ties, shared all property equally, and followed the leadership of one chief. This loyalty to individual tribes, or clans, remained strong despite the new feudal system. Conflicts, however, soon arose between rival clans and also between Lowland Scots, many of whom supported the king, and Highland Scots, who honored the clan system. Difficulties also increased between Scotland and England, as English kings attempted to extend their rule over Scotland.

THE BORDER REIVERS

The period between the fifteenth and seventeenth centuries was a time of great upheaval for the people living near the Scottish-English border. Many formed outlaw groups and sought their livelihood at the expense of others in the form of cattle rustling, blackmailing, and kidnapping.
(A Closer Look, page 48)

THE WARS OF INDEPENDENCE

In 1290, the question of succession to the Scottish throne brought about conflict between Scotland and England. This tension exploded into the Wars of Independence. The wars were long and bitter but are remembered by the Scots as their greatest victory over the English. The wars resulted in England's recognition of Scotland's independence in 1328.

(A Closer Look, page 72)

Left: This hand-colored woodcut from the *Boke of Surveying* (1523) shows a tenant paying rent to his landlord.

The Stuarts

The Stuarts (also known as the Stewarts) reigned from 1371, when Robert II became king, to Queen Anne's death in 1714. These years were filled with fighting between Scotland and England. In the sixteenth century, however, these struggles were overshadowed by the Protestant Reformation. The rivalry between England's Queen Elizabeth I (r. 1558–1603), a Protestant, and Scotland's Queen Mary Stuart (r. 1542–1567), a devout Catholic and Elizabeth's cousin, resulted in Mary's execution at Fotheringhay Castle, England, in 1587. In 1603, Queen Elizabeth I died, leaving Scotland's King James VI, Mary's son, the legal heir. When James assumed the throne of England, he became King James I of England, while remaining James VI of Scotland. Since then, the reigning monarch of England has also ruled Scotland.

The Era of Union

In 1707, the Act of Union united the Scottish and English parliaments. Scotland became an integral part of the United Kingdom, except in the areas of law, education, and religion. The union meant that Scotland enjoyed free trade with England and England's colonies and prospered as Britain's empire grew.

The union was opposed by many of the Highland Scots, who instigated the Jacobite rebellions of 1708, 1715, and 1745–1746. Their hopes for independence were dashed at the Battle of Culloden in 1746, when the government's army defeated the Jacobite army. Laws passed after the rebellion suppressed the clan system. Forfeited clan holdings became estates owned by government officials and nobles, rather than by clan leaders who were tied to their subjects by blood and tradition.

Eighteenth-Century Scotland

The Industrial Revolution gripped Scotland in the eighteenth century and transformed it from an agricultural to an industrial nation. Scotland's textile industry gained worldwide prominence, while shipbuilding, iron casting, and mining dominated the country's economy.

BONNIE PRINCE CHARLIE AND THE JACOBITE RISINGS

In the eighteenth century, famous attempts were made to replace the king of England, first with James Edward Stuart and then with Charles Edward Stuart, also known as Bonnie Prince Charlie.

(A Closer Look, page 46)

Below: Glasgow flourished during the Industrial Revolution and, by the end of the nineteenth century, had become a major industrial center and a busy port for trade and travel to the Americas.

At the same time, a growing population and scarcity of land for farmers led to poverty in Scotland's farmlands. Many landowners switched from agriculture to fishing and raising sheep, and their tenants no longer had work. The Crofters Holdings Act of 1886 was one attempt to help poor Scots gain some economic security by establishing fair rents, but poverty persisted, and many Scots began to emigrate.

Early Twentieth-Century Scotland

By the end of the nineteenth century, Scottish workers were underpaid and overworked, while managers and owners made great financial gains. The gap between employees and employers increased rapidly. Workers began to demand changes, however, in terms of both wages and general working conditions.

During World War I, Scots worked hard to support the war effort. Ultimately, Scotland paid dearly during the war, as 74,000 Scots died serving their country.

In late 1918, the "Great War" ended, and Scotland's economic worries increased once again. A postwar period of economic depression began in Britain, and Scotland's economy suffered greatly during this time.

Above: **Led by a piper, these Scottish troops left the trenches to the east of Oppy and marched back to their camp in France in March 1918. Many Scottish men signed on at the outbreak of World War I, while others worked in Scotland's shipyards.**

THE SCOTTISH ENLIGHTENMENT

The industrialization of Scotland coincided with the boom of intellectual life referred to as the Scottish Enlightenment. Literature, in particular, blossomed. The Scottish education system also flourished, producing scholars who specialized in single subjects.

The Move toward Devolution

As the economic situation in Scotland worsened during the 1920s, many workers turned to socialism. In 1928, the Scottish Nationalist Party (SNP) was established to seek home rule, a movement now called "devolution." In 1934, the Nationalist Party merged with the Scottish Party to form the Scottish National Party (SNP), which was in favor of self-government. The national government of the 1930s, however, was dominated by the Conservative Party.

With the end of World War II in 1945 and the decline of Britain as a world power, Scottish nationalism once again became a significant political force. In 1979, the government, headed by the Labour Party, called a referendum to approve Scotland's devolution. The move failed, however, because an insufficient number of Scots voted. The Conservative Party elected later that year dropped any further plans for a Scottish government.

With the election of the Labour Party in 1997, hopes for devolution were renewed. British prime minister Tony Blair supported the idea of devolving some of the parliament's powers to national legislatures in Scotland. Seventy-five percent of Scots who went to the polls voted in favor of creating their own parliament. The new Scottish Parliament went into effect in 1999, with Donald Dewar as its First Minister.

Below (left to right): **Lord James Douglas Hamilton; Prince Philip, Duke of Edinburgh; Donald Dewar; Queen Elizabeth II; and Sir David Steel watch the festivities celebrating the opening of the Scottish Parliament in 1999. These ceremonies marked the opening of the first Scottish Parliament in nearly three hundred years.**

Elsie Maude Inglis (1864–1917)

An early advocate of women's rights, Elsie Maude Inglis attended medical school at the Glasgow Royal Infirmary and the Edinburgh School of Medicine for Women. She founded the Scottish Women's Suffrage Federation in 1906. During World War I, she helped establish the Organization of Scottish Women's Hospitals. The Elsie Inglis Maternity Hospital was built in Edinburgh in Inglis's honor after her death in 1917.

Elsie Maude Inglis

John Knox (c. 1514–1572)

Known as the Father of Presbyterianism, John Knox, a former Catholic priest, took up the Protestant cause in Scotland in 1547. Knox, however, was captured by Scottish regent Mary of Guise's French troops in mid-1547 and was forced into service as a galley slave. Upon his release in 1551, Knox went into the service of the English king, Edward VI. In 1559, he returned to Scotland and began an extended protest against the reign of the Catholic queen, Mary of Scots. After Mary was beheaded in England, Knox persisted with his religious reformation. He eventually established his own style of Protestantism, named *Presbyterianism*, which is the major religion in Scotland today.

John Knox

Sir Alexander Fleming (1881–1955)

Son of a Scottish sheep farmer, Alexander Fleming was a talented bacteriologist. While working with *staphylococcus* bacteria in 1928, Fleming accidentally left a culture dish smeared with the bacteria on his desk. While he was on vacation, mold spores began to grow in the dish. The bacteria also grew but not in the area covered by the mold. When Fleming returned, he realized that something in the mold had prevented the growth of the bacteria. The unknown ingredient had even killed the bacteria. Fleming named this bacteria-fighting element in the mold *penicillin*. In 1944, Fleming received a knighthood. The following year, he was awarded the Nobel Prize for Physiology or Medicine, along with British biochemist Sir Ernst Boris Chain and Australian pathologist Howard Walter Florey. Sir Alexander Fleming died in 1955 and was buried in St. Paul's Cathedral, London.

Sir Alexander Fleming

Government and the Economy

System of Government

In 1999, Scotland's governmental system underwent a major change, and a Scottish parliament was reestablished. The Scottish Parliament is located in Edinburgh and has 129 members. First Minister Henry McLeish is the leader. Now, Scotland can act on many important issues that directly affect its own people, including health, housing, and economic development.

Besides having its own parliament, in which democratically elected men and women represent the interests of the constituencies that voted for them, Scotland is still represented by seventy-two ministers of parliament (MPs) in the House of Commons in London. These MPs sit in the larger British Parliament and vote on actions and laws that affect the entire United Kingdom, not just Scotland. For now, the parliament in London remains in charge of national and international policies and decisions related to Scotland's military and defense, foreign affairs, taxation, and economic policy.

FROM UNION TO DEVOLUTION

The Act of Union of 1707 formally joined the Scottish and English parliaments so that most laws affecting Scotland were decided upon in the House of Commons in London. Over time, Scotland grew frustrated with its inability to produce legislation in its own best interest. In the 1970s, proposals were introduced to transfer, or devolve, more powers to the Scottish government. Twenty years later, devolution was finally achieved.

Left: Members of Scottish Parliament (MSPs) are sworn in during the historic first day of the Scottish Parliament in Edinburgh on May 12, 1999.

As Scotland is still part of the United Kingdom, Queen Elizabeth II serves as the head of state, while British prime minister Tony Blair is the current Head of Parliament. John Reid, the present secretary of state for Scotland, acts as intermediary between the interests of Scotland and the larger U.K. government.

On a regional level, Scotland is divided into areas called unitary, or local, authorities. The governmental bodies have limited powers to manage their own localities and are in charge of economic development, housing, and emergency services.

Below: **The new Scottish Office building in Victoria Quay, Edinburgh, was completed in 1996. The building was designed to maximize the use of natural light.**

THE SCOTTISH OFFICE

The Judiciary System

The Scottish judiciary system is based on civil law, which is derived from ancient Roman law, whereas the rest of Britain follows common law, which originated in England. The Court of Session is Scotland's highest ranking court and handles civil matters. The lord president is the head of the Court of Session. The High Court of Justiciary is Scotland's supreme criminal court. Cases are tried by a judge and a jury of fifteen people. The lord justice general is the leading judge of the High Court.

Scotland is also divided into six areas called sheriffdoms. Within these sheriffdoms are forty-nine sheriff courts. Most cases are heard before a judge, called a sheriff, who deals with civil and criminal cases of a less serious nature.

THE ROLE OF THE EUROPEAN PARLIAMENT

Issues relevant to Scotland and the rest of the United Kingdom, such as consumer protection and trade agreements, are reviewed by the European Parliament in Brussels, Belgium. The European Parliament has the authority to regulate issues that have an impact on the European Union (EU) as a whole.

Economy

During the Industrial Revolution of the eighteenth and nineteenth centuries, power-driven machinery and heavy industry, including coal and iron ore mining, altered Scotland's economy and created new jobs. The nation became a leading producer of cotton and textiles as well as iron and steel. Trade and shipbuilding also increased dramatically.

After World War I, however, a worldwide economic depression almost destroyed Scotland's major industries. In the second half of the twentieth century, the Scottish economy slowly began to recover.

Farming, fishing, and sheepherding have long been practiced in Scotland. Scotland is known for its beef and dairy cattle and for its dairy products. About one-fourth of Scotland's land is used for agriculture. The most important crops are wheat, barley, and potatoes. Scotland's shellfish and fishing industries make up more than two-thirds of the United Kingdom's total annual catch and contribute significantly to the world's food supply. Haddock, cod, and herring are among the most common fish species landed in Scottish ports. Forestry is also an important industry, and its expansion has helped the rural economy prosper.

OIL IN THE NORTH SEA

Every evening after dark, lights glitter in the waters off the coast of Aberdeen. Some of the lights guide fishing boats, but many are stationary and permanently lit. Twenty-four hours a day, large rigs hunt for and pump crude oil. Today, the North Sea is one of the world's richest sources of oil and natural gas, and Aberdeen is Scotland's headquarters for the industry.
(*A Closer Look, page 56*)

Below: **The island of Iona in the Inner Hebrides provides an ideal location for sheep farming.**

Above: **The former Templeton Carpet Factory has been transformed into one of Glasgow's bustling business centers.**

Due to foreign competition and changes in demand, the production of coal, steel, and iron has declined over recent years, and the closing of many plants has led to fewer jobs. Unemployment is a serious problem in Scotland, especially in areas where major industries were based.

Following the move away from heavy industry, attempts have been made to restructure and modernize Scotland's economy. Glasgow, the country's second largest city, has evolved from an industrial center into a major seaport and shipbuilding locality and is also the center for many high-technology industries. Since the discovery of oil and natural gas in the North Sea in the 1970s, Aberdeen has become one of Europe's major petrochemical centers.

Scotland's main exports include electronics, personal computers and software, office equipment, semiconductors, and automated teller machines. Scotland is also a leader in biotechnology. Other major exports include textiles, oil and natural gas, paper, salmon, and whiskey. Sixty percent of Scotland's manufacturing products are exported to Europe. Major trade partners include Germany, France, Russia, the United States, Canada, Brazil, and Japan.

SCOTLAND'S AIRPORTS

Scotland is served by three airports. Situated near a major oil-producing area, Aberdeen Airport features the world's largest heliport and provides regular helicopter service to the offshore oil rigs. Serving the capital of Scotland, Edinburgh Airport not only handles passengers but is also a major airfreight center. Glasgow Airport is a main hub for travelers from overseas, especially from the United States.

People and Lifestyle

The Scots are known for their keen sense of humor, their nationalistic pride, and their love of their homeland. Over the centuries, people from different backgrounds have married in Scotland and created a population that is culturally and ethnically diverse. In recent decades, Scotland has attracted immigrants, not only from elsewhere in the United Kingdom and continental Europe, but also from India, Pakistan, Southeast Asia, North America, New Zealand, and Australia.

Below: **This croft is located in Balallan on Lewis Island. Peat piled up at the back of the house is used as fuel during the long winter months.**

The Scottish Lifestyle

Historically, Highlanders and Lowlanders have been devoted to their respective sections of Scotland, to their own living patterns, and to their own particular causes. These differences have frequently led to warfare. Even today, the two groups remain divided by their loyalty to their own regions.

From the late 1700s to the mid-1800s, Scotland's social system was dramatically changed, largely due to a shift from farming to fishing and raising livestock. During these years, large farms were created by combining small properties into massive estates. Many people were forced to move away to find new homes and develop new ways of life. Some Scots emigrated to other countries, such as the United States and Canada, while others migrated to

SCOTTISH CLANS AND THEIR KILTS

With more than 2,500 tartans contained in the *Register of All Known Tartans*, the kilt is the distinctive costume of the Scots.

(A Closer Look, page 60)

manufacturing areas in the Central Lowlands. Some Scots became crofters, or farmers of small plots of land, in the Highlands or on the Scottish islands.

Crofters grow their own grain or vegetables but raise animals with several other crofters on a large grazing area. Individual crofts range in size from 12 acres (5 hectares) to 123 acres (50 hectares). As a result, some crofters only have enough work for about two days per week. In order to survive and feed themselves and their families, crofters usually have two or more jobs, including fishing, teaching, or working in the tourist industry. Today, as many as 12,000 men and women work

Below: **Dressed in traditional Scottish attire, a grandfather and grandson enjoy the beautiful scenery of the Highlands.**

as crofters and experience a strong sense of community. Although many young people decide to move away to try something more profitable or rewarding, crofting remains a way of life.

Poverty exists both in cities and rural areas, despite the overall high level of employment. Of the 800,000 people who are on some form of income support, or welfare, about half are children. During the 1990s, one in three people experienced poverty in rural areas, and many Scots could not find decent housing. The lack of reliable public transportation often prevents people from traveling to cities to work.

In rural Scotland, tourism has overtaken farming as a major source of employment, while government agencies, such as the health or education systems, provide over one-fourth of all jobs.

SCOTTISH INVENTIONS

Throughout the centuries, Scottish inventors have provided the world with many ingenious items that have become part of our daily lives.
(A Closer Look, page 64)

21

Family Life

Tradition plays a strong role in Scottish family life. Along with the Scots' love of their homeland comes the love of family and a strong work ethic. Scots are hospitable and enjoy entertaining guests. They also value honesty and personal honor.

Scottish families are close-knit. They carry on some traditions, but they also change with the times. In the past, Christmas was a minor holiday, but it now has become more important than New Year in many households. Traditionally, gifts were exchanged at New Year, but, today, many families exchange gifts at Christmas.

Most parents insist that their children obtain a good education. As a result, many children move away to attend a university and to find work, but they return regularly to enjoy the comforts of home. Children are taught to work. It does not matter what job they do; it is the act of working that is important. Scots also value courtesy, respect their elders, and encourage their children to be proud of their Scottish heritage. Most Highland family members know Scottish dances and other traditions, and some Scots speak Gaelic.

CROFTS

A large, extended family can live in one croft house. The house is well-adapted to the harsh climate. Its thatched roof and thick stone walls keep in the warmth during winter and the cool air during summer. Sleeping arrangements are usually cramped. Grandparents, parents, and the youngest children sleep in one room, girls share one bed in another room, and boys sleep in a third room.

Below: **A Scottish family takes a relaxing stroll near a stream in the Central Lowlands.**

Women in Scotland

The women of Scotland have been economically independent since the nineteenth century, when many were employed in the textile and fish-processing industries. In recent years, women have been entering universities and the professions in increasing numbers. This economic and intellectual independence gives them a high degree of authority within the family.

Of the entire female workforce, only 52 percent work full-time. Scottish women often work as secretaries, clerks, or teachers, or in shops, hotels, restaurants, health and social services, or financial and business services. The number of women officers in the Scottish police force is rising. Despite equal-pay laws, however, women in Scotland still only earn about three-quarters of men's average salaries. Women are also more likely than men to live at the poverty level, and some cannot go to work because they cannot afford child care.

Over one-third of the new Scottish Parliament is made up of women. Of the 129 Members of Scottish Parliament (MSPs), forty-eight are women, about 37 percent of the entire membership.

Above: This woman in a factory in Dundee is weaving wool on a loom that produces Johnston's cashmere.

GRETNA GREEN

Gretna Green, near the border with England, is Britain's "wedding capital." In the past, girls as young as twelve came from outside Scotland to Gretna Green to marry their sweethearts under the easier conditions of Scottish law. Today, both bride and groom must be sixteen years of age to have a civil ceremony. Many people still journey to Gretna Green to tie the knot because of its romantic history.

Education

All Scots between the ages of five and sixteen must attend school. Public schools are free, and parents have the right to choose which school their children attend. Schools do not follow a national curriculum, but the Scottish Office Education and Industry Department monitors closely what is taught. Parents take active roles in their children's education and participate in the development and implementation of school policies.

Formal Schooling

Students between the ages of five and twelve attend elementary school for seven years. Besides reading, writing, and arithmetic, students are encouraged to express themselves through art and music and participate in physical exercise. Courses also include environmental studies, religion and morality, and languages. A special Gaelic-language program is available for students living in the Highlands, the Western Isles, and parts of central Scotland.

After elementary school, students attend junior high school. Students study English, mathematics, science, social studies, and a foreign language until the age of sixteen.

After four years of junior high school, students take an examination to qualify for the Scottish Certificate of Education, or Standard Grade. Those who pass go on to senior high school

SCHOOL SPORTS

Students participate in a wide variety of sports during elementary and high school. Apart from fitness sports, such as swimming, walking, and aerobics, the most popular activities are soccer, cycling, snooker, golf, dance, and weight training. Other school sports include rugby, tennis, ice hockey, shinty, basketball, volleyball, and netball.

Left: These students are on their way home after school on the island of Skye.

Left: The University of Saint Andrews, in northeastern Fife, is Scotland's oldest university, dating to 1411. The university has an international reputation for its excellent under-graduate and post-graduate programs as well as for its important work in the field of research. It is one of Scotland's fourteen universities.

for one or two years. After the first year of senior high school, students take about five examinations. These examinations permit entrance to a university. About 7 percent of Scottish students choose to go on to a college at this point, while the remainder attend another year of senior high school. At the end of the sixth year of post-elementary school, students take examinations for their Certificates of Sixth Year Studies (CSYS), which are necessary if they wish to attend a university in England.

Higher Education

About half of young Scots enroll in higher education courses. Currently, Scotland has twenty-three institutions of higher learning. Students may either obtain a three-year ordinary degree or continue their studies for another year to attain an honors degree.

Students who do not attend a university are encouraged to participate in lifelong learning programs. Many choose further education programs, in which they may gain job-related skills or receive preemployment training sponsored by some industries.

YOUTH OUT-MIGRATION

Frequently, students who leave school at sixteen have difficulty finding work in Scotland. Those who do work are usually paid very low wages. By the age of nineteen, many young people, especially those living in the Scottish Borders, migrate to other parts of the United Kingdom, seeking employment or a better standard of living. Within four years of leaving home, these "out-migrants" usually find suitable work or enroll at a university.

Left: This stained glass window in Iona Abbey shows Saint Columba. Saint Columba settled on the island of Iona in 563 with the aim of converting Celtic tribes in Scotland to Christianity. Restoration of the abbey was completed in 1965.

Religion in Scotland

Scotland's official religion is the Presbyterian Church of Scotland. Roman Catholicism is widely practiced and is the second largest religion. A few Presbyterian sects that separated from the Church of Scotland are also present. Minority religions exist, and Glasgow has several synagogues and mosques and a Buddhist center.

For centuries, conflict raged between followers of Roman Catholicism and followers of Protestantism. Christianity first arrived in Scotland with the Celtic Saint Ninian in the fifth century. By the eleventh century, Roman Catholicism began to replace Celtic Christianity as Scotland's main religion.

The Protestant Reformation in the sixteenth century led to Scotland's break from the Roman Catholic Church. Led by John Knox, Scottish reformers held a parliament in August 1560 and abolished the authority of the pope. A century of religious strife ended in 1689 after William of Orange (r. 1689–1702) and Mary (r. 1689–1694) defeated James II in the Glorious Revolution and became the English monarchs. Presbyterianism was then officially established in Scotland.

SAINT MARGARET AND KING DAVID I

Margaret of Scotland (c. 1045–1093), who was declared a saint in 1250, was largely responsible for encouraging Scots to adopt Catholicism. During the twelfth century, her son King David I continued his mother's work and invited Roman Catholic monks from major religious institutions in feudal France to set up communities in Scotland. These monastic orders had a major impact on Scotland and built impressive monasteries, such as the abbeys at Kelso and Melrose in the Borders region.

In the early eighteenth century, the Church of Scotland was split by the Moderates, who were interested in social activities and cultural matters, and the Evangelicals, who were more interested in preaching their religion. The Evangelicals broke away from the Church of Scotland in 1843 and established the Free Church of Scotland. In 1900, the Free Church of Scotland united with the United Presbyterian Church, which had broken away from the Church of Scotland in 1847. Together they formed the United Free Church. The United Free Church reunited with the Church of Scotland in 1929. Those followers who were opposed to the union continued as the Free Church of Scotland.

At the end of the twentieth century, approximately 10 percent of Scotland's population attended church regularly. Today, about one million Scots, or 20 percent of the population, belong to the Church of Scotland, and 750,000 Scots, or 15 percent of the population, are Roman Catholics. Other leading Christian denominations include the Episcopal Church of Scotland, the Free Church of Scotland, Baptists, Congregationalists, Methodists, and Unitarians. Other religions include Judaism, Islam, Buddhism, and Baha'i.

CHURCH AND COMMUNITY

Until recently, the local church was the center of life in rural communities, due to their isolation from larger towns and cities. People not only attended church to share their religious beliefs, but they also went to socialize.

Below: Glasgow Cathedral, as it stands today, was completed in 1508. It is the only Scottish mainland medieval cathedral to have survived the Reformation.

Language and Literature

Although English is the official language of Scotland, two other languages are also spoken in the country. *Gaelic* (GAY-lik), a Celtic language sometimes known as Scottish Gaelic outside Scotland, is mainly spoken in the Highlands and the Hebrides, while *Scots* can be heard in southern Scotland.

Gaelic came to Scotland when the Scots arrived from Ireland in about 500. The language spread rapidly, and, by the eleventh century, Gaelic was Scotland's primary language. After the last Jacobite rising in 1745–1746, the British government banned the language in an attempt to divide the loyalties of Highland clans and to unite the nation under British rule. Today, 70,000 people, or 1 percent of the population, can speak Gaelic.

Although Scots sounds similar to English, it is, in fact, a separate language. Also known as *Lallans* (LAH-lanz), Scots is a combination of Old English, or Anglo-Saxon; Norman-French; and Norse. Up until the fifteenth century, the language was called "Inglis" and was used mainly to write literature and to keep official records. By the nineteenth century, English had taken over as the most popular language, and many writers began to use Scots intentionally to prevent it from disappearing. Nevertheless, Scots never witnessed the revival that Gaelic did.

THE GAELIC REVIVAL

Efforts have been made to halt the decline of Gaelic language and culture. Founded in 1891, An Comunn Gaidhealach, or the Gaelic Society, organizes the annual Royal National Mod. The Mod celebrates Gaelic culture by holding competitions in singing, poetry, music, and other forms of entertainment. In the 1970s, Sabhal Mór Ostaig, a Scottish Gaelic college, was founded on the island of Skye. Recently, the Scottish government made the promotion of Gaelic a top priority and is now taking steps to give legal status to the language.

Left: Sitting on a bench in Holyrood Park, Edinburgh, this couple leisurely reads *Scotland on Sunday.*

Scotland has had its fair share of important writers who have created some of the world's finest literature. *The Bruce* (1375), by John Barbour (c. 1325–1395), is one of Scotland's oldest poems and is the first major work of Scottish literature. Written in Scots, it tells the story of Robert Bruce and his involvement in the Wars of Independence. Sir Walter Scott (1771–1832) also used Scots to give his novels and poetry a traditional sound. His most famous works include *Waverley* (1814), *Rob Roy* (1818), and *Ivanhoe* (1819). Scotland's national poet, Robert Burns (1759–1796), wrote the lyrics of many popular tunes, including *Auld Lang Syne*.

Twentieth-century writers played major roles in reviving both Gaelic and Scots. Sorley MacLean (1911–1996) wrote in Gaelic about poverty, war, and the struggles for survival in the Highlands. The writings of Hugh MacDiarmid (1892–1978) reflected the socialist movement of the 1920s and kept the Scots language alive.

Other Scottish writers include Sir James Matthew Barrie (1860–1937), who wrote *Peter Pan* (1904); James Alfred Wight (1916–1995), better known as James Herriot, whose stories about veterinary life became a popular television series called *All Creatures Great and Small*; and Sir Arthur Conan Doyle (1859–1930), who created the world's most famous detective, Sherlock Holmes.

Above: **Scottish poet Robert Burns (*left*) transformed the traditional folk songs of Scotland into great poetry and immortalized its countryside and humble farm life. Sir Walter Scott (*right*) was a major historical novelist. In Great Britain, he created an enduring interest in Scottish traditions.**

ROBERT LOUIS STEVENSON

Author of novels such as *Treasure Island* (1883) and *The Strange Case of Dr. Jekyll and Mr. Hyde* (1886), Robert Louis Stevenson is famous for his adventure stories about buried treasure and pirates.

(A Closer Look, page 70)

Arts

Music

Scotland's music reflects its ancient past as well as the influence of modern styles, including rock and jazz. The folk roots of Scottish music give it a special sound, and the Gaelic language greatly influences much of Scotland's national music. Runrig, a band that uses strong Gaelic lyrics, has popularized the ancient language with its songs, its use of accordions and bagpipes, and its modern rock style. Celtic origins are also identifiable in the music of Capercaillie, one of Scotland's most popular bands.

Some Scottish music, such as *ceilidh* (KAY-lee) music, is directly associated with dancing. Ceilidh music is often heard at weddings or other celebrations. Today, a more modernized version of this music is taking hold in Scotland and tends to be informal and improvised. Bands such as the Benachally Ceilidh Band have popularized this exciting music.

In the world of rock music, Scottish performers include Garbage's Shirley Manson; Jethro Tull's vocalist and flutist Ian Anderson; and the Eurythmics's Annie Lennox. Well-known Scottish groups include Texas, Wet Wet Wet, Simple Minds, and the Bay City Rollers.

Left: Evelyn Glennie, a Scottish musician, is committed to bringing solo percussion music to a wider audience. To date, she has had twenty-three percussion concertos and many more recital pieces commissioned for her throughout her illustrious career.

Opposite: Young girls dance to the sound of bagpipes during a street celebration in Edinburgh, the capital of Scotland.

Evelyn Glennie, on the other hand, is an accomplished classical musician. She has won many awards with her incredible talent as a solo percussionist, including a Grammy Award in 1988 and the Order of the British Empire (OBE) in 1993. Glennie also plays the great Highland bagpipe. What makes her success even more impressive is that she is completely deaf.

Dancing

Traditional Scottish dancing dates back to the eleventh century, when it developed as a way to celebrate victory over the enemy. Requiring incredible skill and concentration, Highland dancing also became an important training technique for soldiers who were preparing for war. Highland dancing is performed to the sound of bagpipes.

Scottish country dancing and ceilidh dancing are also popular among Scots. Introduced to Scotland in the eighteenth century, country dancing is similar to ceilidh dancing, as both involve six to ten couples dancing to strict routines. A caller, however, shouts out the steps in a ceilidh.

SCOTTISH DANCING

Traditional Scottish dances, such as the Highland Fling, take months of practice to master.
(A Closer Look, page 62)

PLAYING THE BAGPIPE

Bagpipes are the most recognizable of Scotland's musical instruments. Their droning frequently accompanies traditional Highland dances. For centuries, the pipes and drums have led Scottish soldiers into battle, stirring fear into the hearts of their enemies.
(A Closer Look, page 58)

Architecture

Prehistoric villages, such as Skara Brae in the Orkneys, as well as Charles Rennie Mackintosh's unique, modern Scottish architecture of the early twentieth century, are equally distinctive in Scotland's landscape.

During the Bronze and Iron Ages, a variety of structures were built in Scotland. These hill forts, crannogs, and brochs still dot the countryside. During the Middle Ages, castles began to dominate the land, as did monasteries and churches associated with the Celtic Christian and Roman Catholic religions. The tower house, a special type of Scottish castle, was developed in response to conflicts between clans and families throughout Scotland and to the threat from England.

The eighteenth century in Scotland was called the Scottish Enlightenment. Scientific and intellectual life flourished, and many well-known writers and artists date from this time. Two great Scottish architects were Robert Adam (1728–1792) and James Gibbs (1682–1754). Adam was known for his innovative neoclassical style, while Gibbs's style tended to be more classically Roman.

Below: **Floors Castle is the largest inhabited castle in Scotland and is the home of the Duke and Duchess of Roxburghe. Built by Scottish architect William Adam (1689–1748) in 1721 and modified by Scottish architect William Playfair (1789–1857) in the nineteenth century, the castle stands among thousands of acres (hectares) of park and woodlands overlooking the River Tweed.**

Left: **The home in which Charles Rennie Mackintosh and his wife, Margaret MacDonald, lived from 1906 to 1914 adjoins the University of Glasgow's Art Gallery. The Mackintosh Gallery is located in the upper level.**

Nineteenth-century British architecture tended toward heavy, Gothic styles, but more modern art forms developed in the twentieth century. Charles Rennie Mackintosh (1868–1928); his wife, Margaret MacDonald; her sister, Frances; and Frances's husband, Herbert MacNair, joined together to create what became known as "the Glasgow Style." Mixing traditional Scottish architecture with art nouveau and Japanese art, they developed a distinctive architectural style. Examples include the Mackintosh House and the Lighthouse, both located in or around Glasgow.

Modern Scottish architecture now emphasizes glass and geometric designs and can be seen at the Royal Botanic Garden in Edinburgh and Glasgow's Burrell Collection. Each decade sees a movement toward new styles, but all periods of Scotland's architectural heritage retain key parts of the nation's culture.

Painting

Among the most important contributions to Scottish painting is the work of four Glasgow artists called "the Scottish Colourists." Working at the beginning of the twentieth century, Samuel John Peploe (1871–1935), Francis Campbell Boileau Caddell (1883–1937), George Leslie Hunter (1877–1931), and John Dunce Fergusson (1874–1961) painted in bright, bold colors. These painters were influenced by the French artists Édouard Manet (1832–1883) and Henri Matisse (1869–1954). The works of the Scottish Colourists were praised internationally, and they continue to influence contemporary painters.

SCOTTISH ART

Most Scottish artists have developed their own styles while studying at one of the country's four art colleges, namely Edinburgh College of Art, Glasgow School of Art, Duncan of Jordanstone College of Art in Dundee, and Grays School of Art in Aberdeen. Scottish potters, painters, and sculptors create a wide range of objects, many of which are sold in the art galleries located in Scotland's major cities.

JOAN EARDLEY

Joan Eardley (1921–1963) is regarded as one of the greatest Scottish artists of the second half of the twentieth century. Her paintings of children in Glasgow and seascapes and landscapes of Catterline reflect the essence of Scottish life.

33

Leisure and Festivals

Leisure Activities

Modern-day Scots enjoy social activities that involve family and friends. They also thrill to the physical exertion that comes with exploring the great outdoors. Scotland is well known as a popular destination for walkers, and, on most days, people can be seen walking the Central Lowland moors and the rugged hills of the Highlands. One of the most popular leisure activities is hill walking, which involves hiking to lower level hills and trekking up one of Scotland's 284 mountains over 3,000 feet (914 m) high, collectively known as the Munros.

Scotland has several national hiking trails that are accessible to the public throughout the year. These trails usually crisscross farmland as well as pass through some of the country's most beautiful scenery. Major footpaths include the Speyside Way and the Southern Upland Way. The Ramblers Association and other hiking clubs ensure that these footpaths remain open to anyone who wishes to walk along them.

MUNRO BAGGING

Sir Hugh Munro (1865–1919), a founding member of the Scottish Mountaineering Club, listed all the Scottish mountains over 3,000 feet (914 m) high in his book *Munro's Tables* in 1891. This list has led to the popular leisure activity of Munro bagging. Munro bagging involves attempting to climb all the 284 mountains listed in *Munro's Tables*. Nearly two thousand hill-walking enthusiasts have climbed all the Munros and are known as Munroists.

Left: This family is wrapped up warmly for a leisurely walk in the Highlands during winter. Going for walks is a popular pastime in Scotland.

Above: **Many Scots like to take time out and relax at outdoor cafés.**

Fishing is another outdoor leisure activity that has long been popular with Scots and visitors to Scotland. Scotland is rich in fishing streams, freshwater lakes, and sea lochs and is famous throughout the world for its delicious salmon, as well as sea trout, brown trout, and pike. Each species has a specific fishing season, depending on the region and the time of year. Two of the best rivers for salmon fishing are the Tay and the Dee, but smaller streams also provide homes for these tasty fish.

The local public house, or pub, is often the social center of a town or village. Some pubs act as a hangout for the men of the area, while others serve a more varied crowd of families and mixed groups. The legal drinking age in Scotland is eighteen, but many pubs allow children in their family rooms, if they are accompanied by adults.

Indoor activities include reading, watching television, and listening to music. Families tend to be close-knit and enjoy playing board games, such as tiddledywinks, together. Bingo is also a popular leisure activity.

SHOALS OF HERRING

Herring, a rich source of food in Scotland and elsewhere, is in constant danger of extinction from overfishing. Efforts to control the fisheries and repopulate the species have not been successful.
(A Closer Look, page 68)

Sports

Scots are avid sports fans. They enjoy watching soccer, rugby, curling, and motor sports as well as traditional games, such as shinty and the caber toss. Scots also actively participate in a wide range of activities.

One sport Scotland rightfully claims as its own is golf. Golf was played in Scotland as early as the fifteenth century. The first formal golf club, the Company of Gentlemen Golfers, now the Honourable Company of Edinburgh Golfers, was established in Edinburgh in 1744 and developed the first set of golfing rules. In 1754, a small, private golf club was founded in the Fife region and named the Society of St. Andrews Golfers. The club gained King William IV's patronage in 1834 and was renamed the Royal and Ancient Golf Club of St. Andrews. This club is the official ruling organization of the sport. Today, St. Andrews is considered the home of Scottish golf, and its Old Course has been in use since the 1500s; it is one of over four hundred golf courses in Scotland. Presently, Glasgow-born Colin Montgomerie is at the top of his golf game and is just one of Scotland's many professional golfers.

Soccer is also wildly popular throughout Scotland, and most towns or villages have a soccer team. Scotland's best-known teams are the Rangers Football Club and the Celtic Football Club, whose rivalry dates back to 1888 when Celtic played its first match and beat the Rangers 5-2.

SYDNEY 2000

In the 2000 Olympic Games held in Sydney, Australia, Scottish athletes won three gold medals and six silver medals. Dundee-born Shirley Robertson was the first Scotswoman to win an Olympic gold medal since Isabella Moore in the 1912 Olympic Games in Stockholm, Sweden. Robertson won a gold Olympic sailing medal in the women's European dinghy class, while Moore won the 100-meter free-style swimming event.

Below: Recognized the world over as the "Home of Golf," St. Andrews is a world-famous golf course. International golfers tend to boast if they have played here or on other prestigious Scottish courses.

Curling is an unusual sport that was possibly invented in Scotland. The first recorded curling event in Scotland dates back to the early sixteenth century, and the game has been popular ever since. A true winter sport, curling involves two teams of four players; brooms, or brushes; ice; and round stones. One player aims a stone at a circle, called a button, at the opposite end of the ice rink and gives it a push. The other three players on the team sweep snowy fragments of ice out of the path of the stone so that it has a smooth run to the button. The object of the game is for each team to get its stones closest to the center of the button. Each player pushes two stones, and a team can score up to eight points. Blocking and knocking out an opponent's stone are important strategies in this game.

SHINTY

A fast game of skill, shinty is a stick–and–ball sport that has its roots in years gone past.
(A Closer Look, page 66)

Left: A group of adults participates in a friendly game of curling on a frozen lake in the Highlands. Scotland is credited with promoting the game worldwide.

Below: Born in Milton in 1939, Jackie Stewart is regarded by many as one of the most successful and most popular automobile racers in the history of the sport. He is an outspoken supporter of increased safety in racing, both in the cars and on the track.

Formula One Racing and Jackie Stewart

In the world of car racing, Scotland has long been associated with Jackie Stewart. Known as "the Flying Scot," Stewart won the World Drivers Championship in 1969, 1971, and 1973 and had twenty-seven Grand Prix wins during his Formula One career.

In 1997, Stewart returned to racing as the chairman of his own Formula One motor racing team. For his accomplishments, he has been awarded the OBE and is a member of the International Motorsports Hall of Fame.

Major Festivals

Tradition and Scottish pride frequently combine to create some of the country's most entertaining festivals. The Edinburgh Military Tattoo held each year in August is one of Scotland's best-known festivals and brings together some of the world's most talented and famous pipe and drum bands. The Edinburgh International Festival is held at the same time of the year and is one of the world's most important arts festivals. Its Fringe Theatre claims to be the largest in the world with over five hundred performers.

Most Scottish towns and villages have at least one local festival every year. Among the most popular of Scotland's festivals are the many Highland Games and clan gatherings that occur not only in the Scottish Highlands but also in the Lowlands and Scottish Borders. Highland dancing, athletics, and clan meetings are the highlights of these events. The royal family usually attends the annual Royal Braemar Gathering held near their castle at Balmoral.

Hogmanay, celebrated at New Year, is immensely popular. An ancient holiday that dates back at least to the sixteenth century and probably originated centuries earlier, Hogmanay in

THE HIGHLAND GAMES

Legend has it that the Highland Games have been around for about one thousand years. The games give participants a chance to show their skill, strength, and stamina, as well as an opportunity to compete in uniquely Scottish events, such as tossing the caber.
(A Closer Look, page 52)

Below: **Bagpipers stand at attention outside the walls of Edinburgh Castle, preparing to begin a procession through the streets of the capital.**

38

Gaelic is called *Oidche Challainn* (EYE-shee-ah KHAH-lin), which means "evening of the oatcake." Traditionally, visitors took gifts of oatmeal cakes to their friends or relatives to bring them good luck in the new year. The first person to enter a house after midnight on New Year must be dark-haired and is supposed to carry coal, shortbread, salt, a black bun, and a bottle of whiskey. This custom is called "first footing," and the gifts ensure that the house stays warm and its inhabitants have plenty of food and drink for the forthcoming year.

Burns Night takes place on January 25 and honors the memory of Robert Burns, the famous Scottish poet. Traditions include reciting poems written by Burns, wearing formal attire such as kilts, and eating haggis, a type of sausage that is the Scottish national dish.

One of the most important celebrations in Scotland is Halloween on October 31. Scottish children dress up in fancy-dress costumes and go from door to door, asking for candy or money. Before they receive a treat, the children must sing a song or recite a poem. Saint Andrew's Day honors Scotland's patron saint and is celebrated on November 30.

FIRE FESTIVALS

Fire ceremonies play a major role in the celebration of Scottish festivals and draw on Scotland's Celtic and Viking heritage.
(A Closer Look, page 50)

Food

Scotland is a country rich in natural resources, and Scottish food tends to be associated with the land and the sea. Scottish food is simple, yet tasty and distinctive.

Butchers sell the freshest meats, including Aberdeen Angus beef, which is famous for its rich flavor. Other favorite Scottish meats include venison, lamb, and mutton. Of the game birds, grouse is most sought-after and is often served with a bread sauce.

Fish is also a favorite food, especially smoked and fresh salmon, for which Scotland has achieved an international reputation. Brown trout is usually coated in oatmeal and fried with bacon. Families often eat Arbroath smokies (wood-smoked haddock) or have Lochfyne kippers (salted herring) with their breakfasts. Shrimp, mussels, scallops, and lobsters are commonly served in coastal villages.

Scots also enjoy bannocks, barley and oat flour biscuits eaten with cheese; stovied tatties, an onion and potato dish; and colcannon, made from boiled cabbage, carrots, turnips, and potatoes. Skirlie is a casserole dish made from oatmeal, onions, and wild thyme. Scotch broth is often known as "hotch-potch" and consists of a bit of meat on a bone and diced vegetables.

THE WATER OF LIFE

Scotland is one of the world's greatest producers of high-quality malt whiskey. It is called *uisge beatha* (OOSH-kee-ah BEH-er) in Gaelic, which means "the water of life." Known to date back to the fifteenth century, whiskey distilling in Scotland has undergone many changes over the years. Today, each region in Scotland boasts a distinct flavor, based on variations in water and peat used to boil the mixture of yeast, barley, and water. The most famous distilleries include Glenfiddich and Glenmorangie.

Left: **Chefs Tony Singh and Rebecca Burr proudly display a tray of cooked lobster.**

Haggis

Haggis is extremely popular among Scots and is perhaps the best-known Scottish delicacy. Haggis is a kind of sausage made with sheep's entrails, oats, suet, pepper, and onion. The mixture is stuffed into a sheep's stomach bag. The bag is then sewn closed and boiled for up to three hours. Haggis is usually served with vegetables and mashed potatoes.

Left: Uncooked haggis is on display in the window of a butcher's shop in Pitlochry. People either adore or detest the taste of haggis. Scottish poet Robert Burns loved it and even wrote a poem in its honor entitled "Address to the Haggis."

Eating in Scotland

Scots enjoy a hearty breakfast. Traditional breakfasts include sausage, bacon, and eggs, and a choice of potato scones; porridge (served with salt); oatcakes; a buttery, which is similar to a croissant; or black pudding, a cakey sausage patty. Tea with milk is the drink of choice, but coffee is also popular.

Late in the afternoon, between 5:00 and 6:30 p.m., Scots frequently satisfy their hunger with high tea, which consists of a cooked meal and an assortment of cakes and baked goods, including black buns and shortbread. The daily evening meal is generally eaten very late, sometimes after 9:00 p.m.

Fast foods are becoming increasingly available throughout Scotland, at least in large towns and cities. Fish and chip shops, called "chippies," can be found almost everywhere; their menus include fried fish, haggis, and oatmeal-coated puddings. Pizza shops are popular, and cafés commonly serve homemade meals.

SCOTTISH CHEESES

Scots enjoy a variety of regional cheeses. About twenty-five cheesemaking businesses produce Scotland's cheeses. Crowdie, a soft, white cheese rolled in oats when served, is one of the best known. Sometimes, it is flavored with peppercorns or garlic. Bishop Kennedy cheese originated in the medieval monasteries of France and is notable because its rind is washed in whiskey!

A CLOSER LOOK
AT SCOTLAND

Throughout its colorful history, Scotland has witnessed many wars and clashes, including the Wars of Independence and the unsuccessful Jacobite risings of the 1700s. Many of the country's warriors, such as Bonnie Prince Charlie and the bandit Rob Roy, have become legendary, romantic figures.

The diversity of the landscape has also directly influenced Scottish history and the traditions that still shape Scottish lives. Scotland boasts the fascinating Neolithic sites at Skara Brae and the intriguing Standing Stones of Stenness. The disappearance of its herring fisheries and the impact of offshore oil exploration are pressing environmental issues. Scotland has also given rise to many famous people, notably inventors and figures in the arts and sciences. Scottish culture thrives, and Scots still practice age-old traditions, including holding fire festivals, wearing the kilt, playing shinty, and tossing the caber. Each tradition has played a role in shaping modern Scotland.

Opposite: **Brightly colored houses line the harbor of Mull Island in the Inner Hebrides.**

Below: **These fishermen are taking a well-deserved break in their boat moored in Aberdeen harbor.**

The Ancient Orkneys

The Orkney Islands in the North Sea off the northeastern tip of mainland Scotland frequently endure raging storms. In 1850 and 1926, the winds of two particularly ferocious storms uncovered an archaeological site of international importance. The site became known as Skara Brae.

Archaeologists believe Skara Brae was inhabited approximately between 3,200 B.C. and 2,200 B.C. Located on Mainland, the settlement provides unique evidence of daily life in the Orkneys in the late Neolithic era. The storms uncovered a group of seven or eight stone buildings, including a workshop. Archaeologists found that each house contained tables, beds, cupboards, and central fireplaces, all of which were made from stone. Whale jawbones were also discovered. They were probably used to support the thatch roofs, in place of wood from trees, which do not grow on the islands. In the building believed to have been a workshop, fragments of chert, a flintlike rock used to make cutting and scraping tools, were found on the floor. The inhabitants of Skara Brae made pottery decorated with geometric patterns. They probably wore animal skins and beads and pendants made from the teeth and bones of whales and wild boars.

THE HISTORY OF THE ORKNEYS

The Orkney Islands consist of more than seventy islands and islets. The largest island is Mainland, where most of the population lives. The Orkneys were settled by about 4,000 B.C., when farmers established small settlements, fished, hunted, bred livestock, crafted pottery, and built strong stone fortifications and complex burial sites. Bronze and Iron Age peoples also left their mark in the Orkneys, as did the Vikings, who arrived in the eighth century A.D. Viking influences remain today, especially in the local dialects, which combine Scots and Norse words.

Left: Skara Brae lay beneath a sand dune until severe storms in 1850 revealed the ruins. Four buildings were excavated during the 1860s by William Graham Watt, the seventh lord of Breckness Estate. The Neolithic houses were built close to one another and were deliberately covered by a layer of sand, ash, and domestic refuse to provide protection against the weather.

Prehistoric sites can be found almost everywhere on the Orkney Islands. Believed to have been constructed in about 3000 B.C., the Standing Stones of Stenness and the Ring of Brogar are the best known and most impressive of the Orkneys' stone circles. The purpose of these monuments is still unclear. Most scholars agree, however, that they had something to do with a prehistoric religion or belief system.

Elaborate tombs, often called burial chambers, have been excavated as well. Less than one mile (1.6 km) from the Standing Stones of Stenness, Maes Howe barrow is one of Europe's most impressive Neolithic burial mounds and one of the best preserved. Dating to about 2,700 B.C., Maes Howe barrow contains huge slabs of sandstone, some weighing over 3 tons (2.7 metric tonnes), connected together with clay. A central room and three smaller chambers remain intact inside. Except for a piece of a human skull, remains of the ancient dead who were buried here have long since disappeared, probably due to the work of ancient grave robbers. Vikings broke into Maes Howe barrow in the twelfth century and left behind one of the largest collections of runes, an ancient form of writing.

Above: **Located on Mainland, the Ring of Brogar is laid out in a circle, with the stones approximately 6 degrees apart. Of the original sixty stones, twenty-seven remain standing.**

Bonnie Prince Charlie and the Jacobite Risings

For many years, Scotland was the scene of conflict between Roman Catholics and Protestants. In 1685, James VII (r. 1685–1688), a devout Catholic, became king of Scotland and England. (He was known as James II of England). In 1688, however, he fled to France and set up court in exile after being dethroned by William of Orange during the Glorious Revolution of 1688. A Convention of Parliament in 1689 gave the crown jointly to William of Orange and his wife Mary, James's daughter, and excluded James II and his infant son from the succession.

When James II died in 1701, his son, Prince James Francis Edward Stuart (1688–1766), considered himself the rightful heir to the British throne. Known as the Old Pretender, James Edward tried unsuccessfully to reclaim the throne in 1708 and 1715–1716. The latter uprising was known as "the Fifteen." James Edward's supporters were known as Jacobites.

Opposite: **Charles Edward Stuart, the Young Pretender, rides horseback as he enters Edinburgh with his Highland supporters after the Battle of Prestonpans in 1745.**

Below: **A Jacobite (*kneeling*) swears his allegiance to Charles Edward Stuart, the Young Pretender, (*second from right*) during the voyage from France to Scotland in 1745.**

THE GREAT ESCAPE

Following his defeat at Culloden in 1746, the Young Pretender was hunted like a fugitive by the English. He went into hiding in the Hebrides where he was introduced to Flora Macdonald. Disguised as Betty Burke, an Irish spinning maid, the Young Pretender sailed to Skye with Flora and her friends. Flora and the Young Pretender parted as soon as they arrived on the island. When the English found out about her role in the escape, Flora was imprisoned in the Tower of London but was released in 1747.

The high point of the Jacobite movement was the rebellion referred to as "the Forty-Five." In 1745, James II's grandson, Charles Edward Louis Philip Casimir Stuart (1720–1788), known as the Young Pretender or Bonnie Prince Charlie, landed in Scotland to claim the British throne from George II (r. 1727–1760).

Gathering supporters from several clans, Charles took Edinburgh, defeated a British force at Prestonpans, and advanced into England. Support for the Jacobite cause, however, was strong only in the Scottish Highlands, and the Jacobites were soon forced to retreat. Upon their return to Scotland, they faced George II's army at the Battle of Culloden on April 16, 1746. The Jacobite forces were defeated, and Charles fled to France.

With the suppression of "the Forty-Five," the political and religious significance of the Jacobite movement ended. Nevertheless, the movement survived in local sentiment and as a theme in romantic literature. Romanticized through ballads and legends, Bonnie Prince Charlie became a national hero of Scotland.

THE AFTERMATH OF "THE FORTY-FIVE"

The aftereffects of "the Forty-Five" almost wiped out Scottish culture. The Act of Proscription was introduced in 1746, and the Highland Clearances began. Lasting for almost 150 years, some scholars view the Highland Clearances as a form of ethnic cleansing. Historically, however, these clearances were also known as "the Improvements," with the introduction of sheep into the countryside.

The Border Reivers

The Scottish land close to England is known as the Scottish Borders and is separated from England by a natural barrier, the Cheviot Hills. For centuries, the Borders area was the scene of conflict, as both Scotland and England claimed ownership of parts of the borderlands.

Border reivers were outlaw groups that formed as a result of long-standing animosities among clan members and families. Instead of forgiving an injustice or apologizing after an argument, the clan members would split into enemy groups and continue to fight. In fact, the word *feud* comes from the Scots term *feides* (fides) and was applied to the battles between these rival groups. Ultimately, anyone became the enemy, as Scot stole from Scot, and Scots robbed the English. Poverty and starvation partly caused the chaos, not just greed. The reivers defied both the Scottish and English governments and were greatly feared by the Border communities because they were excellent and ruthless fighters.

Below: As early as the thirteenth century, the Borders was an extremely dangerous place, where raiding, thievery, cattle rustling, kidnapping, and even murder were common. Lawlessness and chaos controlled the lives of families living in the Borders, especially in the fifteenth and sixteenth centuries.

Left: Robert "Rob Roy" MacGregor (1671–1734) was a famous Border reiver. His reputation as a Scottish Robin Hood was exaggerated by Sir Walter Scott in his novel *Rob Roy* (1818). MacGregor's life story was made into the 1995 Hollywood film *Rob Roy*, starring Liam Neeson and Jessica Lange.

A reive was an organized raid on a home or farm to steal livestock and possessions. If necessary, reivers kidnapped or killed anyone who interfered, but murder was not normally part of the plan. Stealing cows, horses, and sheep was the primary goal of a reive, and reivers also burned crops. Posses often chased after a band of raiders in a pursuit called "Hot Trod." Raising the hue and cry, everyone in the village between the ages of sixteen and sixty was called to join the Trod; otherwise, they would be labeled traitors.

Once captured, many Border reivers were hanged for their actions. Clans with reputations for reiving were outlawed by the government, but their members continued to raid the countryside. Mary, Queen of Scots, tried to end the lawlessness in the mid-sixteenth century but was unsuccessful. When James VI became King James I of England, he tried to subdue the outlaws, by either executing reivers who were captured or sending them to fight in wars in Europe or into exile in Ireland. The chaos continued well into the mid-seventeenth century, but by then, only a few, close-knit bands were left. In time, even those groups gave up reiving, as there were few places for reivers to hide.

BORDER BALLADS

Border ballads were very popular in the fifteenth and sixteenth centuries. They were spirited heroic tunes that celebrated the raids and feuds that occurred around the Borders. Most ballads dealt with the personal success of individual outlaws and Border reivers rather than events of historic importance. Well-known border ballads include "Jock o' the Side," "Hobie Noble," and "The Bonny Earl of Murray."

Fire Festivals

Neither the Celts nor the Vikings are now considered distinctive ethnic groups in Scotland, but their influence on Scottish culture is still strong. Beginning every New Year, Scotland's Celtic and Viking heritage is celebrated with special fires and festivities around the countryside.

As midnight strikes on Hogmanay, or New Year's Eve, the Flambeaux Festival takes place in Comrie. *Flambeaux* (flam-BOH) is the French word for "beautiful flames." Participants make torches from the branches of birch trees and then line them up along the dyke at the Auld Kirkyaird. At midnight, the torches are set afire, grasped by the men of the village, and lifted high into the air. Then, a procession takes place around Comrie with a pipe band leading the way and followed by the glowing flambeaux. Finally, the men hurl the torches into the River Earn, where they are quickly extinguished.

Below: **While thousands of people greet the New Year by watching the fireworks display above Edinburgh Castle, smaller towns throughout Scotland participate in time-honored fire festivals.**

Above: **Up-Helly-Aa ends in a blaze of glory when the Viking longship is set alight.**

The Burning of the Clavie in Burghead is another fire festival that probably has Celtic origins. Normally, the ceremony happens on January 10 or 11, when villagers cut a barrel in half and fill both halves with tar. The barrel, or clavie, is then mounted on poles, set on fire, and carried around the streets of the town. Burning bits of wood are tossed into doorways. Residents eagerly catch the charred wood and keep it for good luck for the rest of the year. At the end of the procession, the clavie is set onto a mound within the Pictish fort and allowed to burn itself out.

Up-Helly-Aa takes place on the last Tuesday of January in the Shetland Islands, with the largest festival taking place in Lerwick. Originally, Up-Helly-Aa began as a ceremony quite similar to the Burning of the Clavie, with a tar barrel set alight and accompanied by loud partying and fighting. In the 1870s, the festivities were modified due to the chaos that often resulted. A new variation of the ceremony features themes from the Shetlands' Viking past. A model Viking longship called a galley, a long line of torchbearers, and a squad of Vikings called *guizers* (GUY-zers) parade through the streets. Music, dance, and Viking costumes are highlights of the festival, while setting the longship on fire is the main event.

The Highland Games

The Highland Games are popular throughout Scotland. The events require enormous talent, concentration, skill, and bravery. Approximately forty major meetings and gatherings take place yearly. The best known of these games is the Royal Braemar Gathering, in the Grampian region, which is held every September.

Participants compete in standard track and field events, including the long and high jumps, pole vaulting, throwing the hammer, and tossing the weight. In the hammer throwing event, the hammer thrower swings his or her body in an increasingly rapid circle, gaining momentum so that the hammer, a weight on the end of a pole, hurtles a long distance when released. Whoever throws the hammer the farthest distance wins. Tossing a weight for height is another equally difficult event. An iron weight of either 26 or 52 pounds (12 or 24 kilograms) hangs from the end of an iron loop. The athlete grips the loop, then stands almost directly underneath a bar placed overhead. He or she throws the weight, aiming to toss it over the bar without knocking the bar over. Besides gathering enough strength to throw the heavy object overhead, the athlete also has to pay enough attention to avoid dropping the weight on his or her head.

The highlight of the Highland Games is the caber toss, a unique Scottish sporting event that is the strangest-looking and most difficult of all heavy events. The caber is a tapered fir pole about 17 feet (5 m) long and about 90 pounds (40 kg) in weight. The athlete intertwines his or her fingers, grips one end of the caber, and balances it, resting it against his or her shoulder before running full speed ahead. At just the right moment, the athlete lifts the caber into the air. The goal is to throw the caber so that it turns end-over-end and lands with the small end pointing away from the thrower. The best score is given when the caber lands at twelve o'clock, and points are deducted according to the caber's position relative to an imaginary clock.

Anyone can compete in the Highland Games, as the events are not limited to bodybuilders or weightlifters, although they may have an advantage over other competitors. All that is needed to join the events is a bit of skill, a bit of strength, and a lot of endurance.

Above: **This athlete is competing in the weight for distance event at the Rothiemurchas Games in Scotland. In this event, the athlete spins around three times before throwing the weight, which is on the end of a chain, as far as possible.**

THE ORIGINS OF THE HIGHLAND GAMES

Tradition has it that the Highland Games originated in the eleventh century. Used to train men for battle, the competitions increased the men's stamina, strength, and agility and also helped leaders select the best men for war.

Opposite: **This athlete is tossing the caber at the Royal Braemar Gathering. The caber toss is not only difficult but can also be very dangerous, since the logs are heavy and awkward to carry. Sometimes, the caber lands very close to the crowd!**

Loch Ness and Its Monster

Scotland has its fair share of mysteries, none more famous and more puzzling than that of the Loch Ness monster, fondly known as Nessie. Stories of Nessie date as far back as 565, when Saint Columba, credited with introducing Christianity to Scotland, supposedly stopped a monster from attacking a swimmer in Loch Ness. Since then, stories have been told of a strange creature rising out of the dark depths of the icy cold loch, but its existence has never been proven.

Located in the northeastern section of the Great Glen, Loch Ness is a long, narrow, freshwater lake that has the largest volume of fresh water in Britain. Several rivers fill the lake, which is about 23 miles (37 km) long. The jagged, irregular loch drops to a maximum depth of more than 800 feet (243 m).

Modern-day sightings of the Loch Ness monster began in 1933, shortly after a new road was built close to the lake. Since

Below: The ruins of Urquhart Castle overlook Loch Ness. The stronghold dates to the thirteenth century when it was built over the remains of a Pictish fort. The castle fell into ruins after 1689. Some visitors to the castle claim to have seen the Loch Ness monster from the castle walls.

Left: Labeled the "surgeon's picture" by the British press in 1934, Colonel Robert Wilson's picture of the Loch Ness monster was fairly clear and appeared to show the head and neck of a plesiosaurlike creature sticking out of the water. The photograph became the popular image of the Loch Ness monster and was only recently exposed as a hoax.

then, over three thousand alleged sightings of the monster have been reported. Most of the eyewitnesses described a large creature with one or more humps protruding from the loch, while others reported seeing a long neck or flippers.

Since 1958, expeditions have been launched to determine the existence of the Loch Ness monster. Equipped with sonar, a military technology that uses sound to search the underwater environment, each expedition has detected large, moving underwater objects that could not be explained. An expedition carried out in the mid-1970s by the Academy of Applied Sciences of Boston, Massachusetts, produced pictures of an object that looked like the flippers of an aquatic creature.

Theories vary regarding the creature's true nature. Skeptics say the image of a creature in the water is probably nothing more than a floating log or a bird so far away that it is difficult to see clearly. Many others believe that underneath the dark waters lurks a mysterious sea animal, whose ancestors may have been dinosaurs. Scientists who believe in the animal's existence think it may be a descendant of the plesiosaur, an extinct marine reptile. Other scientists maintain that the sea creature is a giant eel or squid.

The Official Loch Ness Exhibition at Drumnadrochit overlooks the lake. All the theories, photos, and evidence are displayed so that visitors may decide for themselves whether or not Nessie really does exist in the cold waters of Loch Ness.

PHOTOGRAPHIC EVIDENCE

Much of the photographic evidence pertaining to the Loch Ness monster remains inconclusive and open to interpretation. After seeing pictures taken during the expedition of the Academy of Applied Sciences of Boston in 1976, Sir Peter Scott, a respected British naturalist, took it upon himself to give the creature the scientific name *Nessiteras rhombopteryx.* This term means "Ness wonder with a diamond shaped fin."

Oil in the North Sea

Discovered in 1970, the North Sea oil reserves have been a major economic boom to Scotland, especially to the city of Aberdeen.

In the 1980s, when North Sea oil production was at its peak, rigs produced 2.6 million barrels of unrefined oil each day. Now some scientists predict that the oil fields contain enough oil to be productive for another thirty to forty years, while others expect the reserves to be depleted much sooner. If the oil industry pulls out of the North Sea, Aberdeen's economy will suffer tremendously. In the mid-1980s, when oil prices dropped from U.S. $80 per barrel to less than U.S. $10 per barrel, Aberdeen experienced a severe depression. Today, the city is financially sound but remains dependent on oil and natural gas production.

Left: **Over one hundred offshore oil rigs, such as this one, are serviced from Scotland. Between eight hundred and nine hundred companies are active in the North Sea.**

THE END OF A RIG

When an oil platform is no longer needed, it is usually brought to shore to be disposed of, recycled, or reused. Removal, however, is not always the best solution. One of the most innovative possibilities is transforming some of the unused rigs into artificial reefs, as investigations have shown that these man-made structures in the North Sea actually attract marine life.

Safety and Environmental Issues

Drilling and pumping oil out of the North Sea presents several environmental and safety problems. The weather is often harsh, with storms creating hazards for workers on the rigs as well as for those flying between Aberdeen and the rigs. Workers occasionally slip into the bitterly cold, shark-infested waters surrounding the giant platforms, and helicopters often get caught in the treacherous winds. Since the North Sea became active in the oil trade, much attention has been paid to making working conditions safe and protecting the men and women who work and live on the platforms. Rig workers attend monthly safety meetings to keep current with the latest information and to review routine safety procedures.

Considerable environmental damage, such as air and water pollution, is caused by drilling and pumping oil from the sea. Despite legal requirements to limit pollution, oil and other chemicals seep into the air and water, and oil spills kill animal and fish populations. Flares from rigs and refineries also contribute to air pollution, so many companies have voluntarily banned flares and use special equipment to avoid having to burn off natural gas.

Oil companies work constantly to meet environmental and safety standards. They recognize that they have a responsibility to the public and to marine life to ensure that oil production is as safe as possible.

Above: Oil supply boats dock in Aberdeen's harbor. The oil and gas industry is vital to the local economy. The industry employs 40,000 people both on- and offshore. Many of the world's largest oil companies, including BP Amoco, Shell, and Texaco, are based in Aberdeen. These companies pour money into Aberdeen's economy, building new facilities, restaurants, and schools. They have also paid for the expansion of the airport and the building of a heliport for helicopters that carry personnel to and from the rigs.

Playing the Bagpipe

No other musical instrument is as Scottish as the blaring bagpipe. For centuries, bagpipers led Scottish armies into battle. Their eerie, shrill sounds were heard for miles (km) over the clanking of swords and the shouts of the fighters. Some experts believe bagpipes were played when clans fought near Perth in 1396, again at the Battle of Harlow in 1411, and near Edinburgh in 1549. They also maintain that Bonnie Prince Charlie's entrance into Edinburgh was announced by the sounds of one hundred pipers during the rebellion of 1745. Other scholars, however, believe that the use of bagpipes for military purposes began much later in the eighteenth century.

Two types of Scottish bagpipes exist. The Lowland bagpipe is blown by a bellows held under the piper's arm, while the Highland bagpipe is blown using the mouth.

Playing the Highland bagpipe, and doing it with skill, is an exceptionally difficult achievement. Beginners start by learning how to play the chanter, or the mouthpiece into which the piper

blows. The task is demanding and requires much discipline to master. It takes a minimum of three to nine months to become accustomed to playing the chanter. Once the chanter is mastered, students progress to the entire set of pipes. They spend another three to nine months developing the stamina to play and learning which fingers go where on the chanter. Most serious students play the bagpipe at least two to five hours a week and join a band after at least one year of practice.

The Edinburgh Military Tattoo

The Edinburgh Military Tattoo brings together many of the world's most talented pipers. Originally, a tattoo was a traditional signal, given with a drum beat, warning soldiers to return to their barracks in the evening. Now, the tattoo has taken on a broader meaning. Each year, military bands consisting of kilted pipers and drummers march across the parade field in front of the city's castle. The setting is reminiscent of past times when pipers led warriors into battle. Even today, almost every military regiment in Scotland has a piper to lead the way.

Above: The Military Tattoo has been held in front of Edinburgh Castle annually in August since 1950. Each year, some 200,000 people from all over the world attend. Watching the display beneath the night skies outside the castle, where kings and queens have lived and struggled since the early Middle Ages, is a unique experience.

Opposite: Performing before an audience, competing at a Highland gathering, or marching in parades or performances are the ultimate goals of any piper.

Scottish Clans and Their Kilts

Scotland's clan system organized people along kinship lines. Each clan had a chief, or kinsman, who was responsible for the welfare of his fellow clan members. Clans were often scattered over a large area and often provided their protection to small groups who became a sept, or branch, of the larger clan. Land ownership was equally divided between all members of a clan.

The kilt, a skirtlike item of clothing, is part of traditional Scottish dress for men. The kilt is comfortable and allows its wearer to move freely. Initially, the patterns on a kilt did not identify the clan. By the late eighteenth century, however, combinations of colors and patterns of plaid began to distinguish a clan's tartan.

Left: These three clansmen are wearing the little kilt, along with all the accessories required for traditional Scottish dress.

THE REVIVAL OF THE KILT

Shortly after the last Jacobite rising was crushed at the Battle of Culloden in 1746, Britain's King George II signed the Act of Proscription. The Act forbade playing the bagpipe, speaking Gaelic, and wearing the kilt. Although the Act was overturned in 1782, it took most Scots another forty years to wear the plaid again. When King George IV visited Edinburgh in 1822, clan chiefs met the king wearing their Highland dress.

Left: **Wearing his clan's tartan, the Duke of Argyll, chief of Clan Campbell, stands on the lawn of his home, Inveraray Castle, in the Central Lowlands.**

The earliest style of kilt, the great plaid, or *feileadh-mór* (EH-leh-mor), consisted of 15 yards (13.7 m) of tartan. The wearer had to spread the cloth on the ground on top of a leather belt. Then, he folded it methodically into pleats and, when finished, lay down on the cloth, gathered the ends, and bound it together with the belt. He pulled one end piece over his shoulder and attached it to the skirt with a brooch.

Nowadays, the great kilt has been replaced with the little kilt, or *feileadh-beg* (EH-leh-beg). This kilt is formed with about 7 yards (6.4 m) of cloth, folded into pleats, then fitted around the waist and fastened at the front with a silver pin. Besides the little kilt, which originated in the mid-eighteenth century, traditional Scottish dress includes a jacket and/or vest made from tweed or wool; a bonnet or a cap adorned with the clan badge, feathers, and a plaid ribbon; a sporran, or a leather purse attached to the waistband; knee-high socks; and a dirk, or dagger, carried at the waist.

Today, the clan system in Scotland is still alive, and the clan chiefs continue the age-old tradition of deciding the pattern and color of the kilts to be worn by their clanspeople. Many chiefs still live in their ancestral castles, such as Blair Castle, belonging to the Dukes of Atholl of Clan Murray.

KILT SKIRTS

The kilt is strictly men's wear, although it is common today to see some women or girls wearing kilts during dance competitions or when playing in pipe bands. Otherwise, women who want to wear their clan's tartan wear a smaller version of the kilt, often called a "kilt skirt." The kilt skirt has about twelve pleats and usually opens from left to right, unlike a man's kilt, which opens in the opposite way. Also, women do not wear bonnets or sporrans, nor do they carry a dirk. Many women prefer wearing a tartan shawl or scarf, attached to a dress with a clan badge.

Scottish Dancing

Whether at a ceilidh or at a festival, you can always expect to enjoy good music and dancing. Scots are famous for the Highland Fling, but this dance is just one traditional form of dance that is popular in Scotland and throughout the world.

Left: **Young girls perform the Sword Dance at a competition during the Royal Braemar Gathering. To touch one of the swords while dancing is considered a sign of bad luck.**

Highland Dancing

The vigorous movements of Highland dancing require the strength of an athlete and the grace of a dancer. Highland dances have remained virtually the same in character over the centuries, but the steps have been refined. The best-known and oldest Highland dance is the Highland Fling, which originated as a victory dance. Now the national dance of Scotland, it was first performed by Malcolm Canmore in 1054 after a battle near Dunsinane. The steps are simple and the tempo uniform. The dancing area is small because the dance was originally performed on a small, round shield carried into battle by a clansman.

The Sword Dance, or *Gillie Callum* (GEE-leh HAL-um), is probably the most exciting of all Highland dances. During the dance, experienced dancers do not look down as they step, arms raised, over and around the tiny spaces formed by crossed swords.

The *Seann Truibhas* (SHAWN trews), which means "Old Trousers," dates to the time just after "the Forty-Five," when Highlanders were forbidden to wear the kilt. The dance celebrates the end of the 1746 Act of Proscription and the renewed opportunity for Highlanders to wear the kilt, rather than trousers. Flowing and graceful steps are first, followed by steps in a quick tempo. The dancer's shaking legs mimic a person shedding his trousers in favor of the native Highland kilt.

Other dances include the Sailor's Hornpipe, in which participants wear sailors' costumes. During the dance, the performers pretend to be on a ship, pulling ropes and watching out for other ships at sea.

Above: **Although Highland dancing is performed mainly by girls, more and more boys are becoming interested in this ancient Scottish tradition. Here, a young boy performs in a Sword Dance competition for beginners during a Highland Games meeting in the Central Lowlands of Scotland.**

Country Dancing

Besides Highland dancing, Scots participate in country dancing. Country dancing consists of couples performing line dances to the tunes, normally, of an accordion. The patterns are similar to square dancing, except that no one calls the steps, and the movements are more restrained.

Competitions and Exhibitions

At Highland Games and gatherings, both Highland dance competitions and country dance exhibitions are popular events. Bagpipes accompany the Highland dancers, while tape recordings often play the tunes for country dancers.

PROMOTING SCOTTISH DANCE

The Royal Scottish Country Dance Society (RSCDS) and the Scottish Official Board of Highland Dancing (SOBHD) were founded in 1923 and 1953, respectively, to promote all types of Scottish dancing. Both of these organizations strive to bring Scottish dance and culture to native Scots and to other people around the world.

Scottish Inventions

From the bicycle to the automobile tire to the telephone, many of the items we use in our daily lives were invented by Scots. Scottish inventors were leading the way as early as 1594, when John Napier (1550–1617) invented mathematical logarithms, sometimes called Napier's Bones. Napier was also the first person to use the decimal point.

During the mid-eighteenth century, Scottish inventors began a revolution that changed the course of modern history. In 1769, James Watt (1736–1819) invented the rotative steam engine by altering an earlier engine to make it work more efficiently. Many historians consider this invention to be singularly responsible for the start of the Industrial Revolution, when engines first powered many factories and mining operations. Watt's name was also adopted for the energy measurement unit, the watt.

Thomas Telford (1757–1834) was an early-nineteenth-century civil engineering genius who designed over 1,200 bridges. His

THE VELOCIPEDE

An early version of one of the world's most popular inventions, the bicycle, was created by Scotsman Kirkpatrick MacMillan in 1839. MacMillan called his device the velocipede. He did not patent his invention, however, and others subsequently copied his design.

Left: James Watt took out his famous patent for "A New Invented Method of Lessening the Consumption of Steam and Fuel in Fire Engines" in 1767, a year after making his first small test engine. Watt was elected Fellow of the Royal Society of London in 1785.

Left: **Alexander Graham Bell (*seated*) tests the telephone that he invented in 1876. While working with deaf students, Bell wondered how electronics and the telegraph system could be combined to send sound signals. Soon, he developed an electronic vibrating machine that transmitted messages using steel reeds, and, from there, he designed the telephone. France awarded Bell the Volta Prize in 1880.**

most famous achievement was Scotland's Caledonian Canal, which linked the country's eastern and western coasts and also several lochs.

Born in Edinburgh in 1847, Alexander Graham Bell emigrated to Canada with his family at the age of twenty-three and invented the first telephone in 1876. He then established the Bell Telephone Company and patented his invention. Bell went on to focus on propellers and air flight and eventually invented the hydrofoil.

Another revolutionary innovation was the television, called a televisor by its Scottish inventor, John Logie Baird (1888–1946). Working in the attic of his London home, Baird used everyday items for his invention, including a tin biscuit box, darning needles, and a bicycle lamp. By 1928, he had refined the televisor so that it could send images across the Atlantic from London to New York City.

The list of Scottish inventions is long and surprising. The pneumatic tire, macintosh raincoats, and marmalade are just a few other common items developed by Scots.

Shinty

While golf is the sport most commonly associated with Scotland, another popular sport is shinty, which many people believe was invented by the Celts hundreds of years ago. Played mainly in the western Highlands, shinty takes its name from the Gaelic word *sínteag* (SHEEN-tee-ak), which means "to skip or leap."

Shinty may have come to Scotland from Ireland about 1,500 years ago. In Ireland, the sport of hurling is very similar to shinty. In the 1850s, Scottish university students thrilled to the game, and its popularity spread quickly. Shinty was formally organized only in the late nineteenth century, however, when a governing body was established and official rules were developed. In 1893, the Camanachd Association was created to ensure the game followed the same rules no matter where it was played. Since then, leagues have been formally established, and competitions are keen.

The ancient sport is played with two teams of twelve players each, including one goalie, for two periods of forty-five minutes

Below: **Scots play a game of shinty in 1845. For decades, playing the game allowed rival villages or Scottish clans to work out their disputes without bloodshed.**

Left: Kingussie's top goal scorer Ronald Ross (*left*) fights for the ball with a Fort William defender (*right*) during the Mactavish Cup Final at Bught Park, Inverness, on April 29, 2000. Fort William beat Kingussie 6-5.

each. The players swing curled wooden sticks, or camans, aiming the triangle-shaped head of the stick at a leather ball and hitting it toward a goal. Like soccer, only the goalkeeper may handle the ball by swatting or stopping it with an open hand. No player may kick the ball. Unlike field hockey, where the sticks and balls are used close to the ground, the sticks in shinty are held over the head, and the ball is hit in the air. To begin a match and start up after a goal and at halftime, the referee tosses the ball at least 12 feet (3.7 m) into the air. Opposing players ready themselves by crossing their camans over their heads. When the ball drops into stick range but is still overhead, players then swing at it.

A goal is scored only when the entire ball crosses over the goal line and passes completely under the crossbar. One point is awarded for each goal. The team with the most goals is the winner. If no goals or an equal number of goals are scored, the game is determined to be a draw.

Shinty can be as chaotic, fast-moving, and dangerous as ice hockey, so safety and courtesy are major concerns. Penalties are given for unsafe play and breaking other rules of the game. The season for shinty occurs about the same time as soccer, and rivalries remain just as fierce as they were in the 1800s.

FIRST SHINTY

Today, boys and girls between the ages of eight and fourteen are encouraged to play a new version of shinty known as First Shinty. The game can be played indoors within a safe environment during winter. In First Shinty, the stick is shorter than an adult's and is made of plastic and rubber. Playing fields are shorter, and a larger, lighter ball is also used, which referees only toss to knee height. Since the ball moves more slowly than in the adult game, new players have more time to develop their skills. The rules have also been simplified to make the game easier to understand.

Shoals of Herring

Scotland is ideally located for fishing, with the North Sea, the Atlantic Ocean, and other bodies of water in and around much of the country. For millennia, these seas and waters have been home to a rich variety of fish, including cod, mackerel, and herring. For just as long, Scotland's fisheries have provided a rich source of food for people. In the North Sea and around the Shetland Islands, where warm currents create an ideal environment for sea life, at least two hundred species of fish thrive.

During the last four hundred years, however, fishing has been so intensive that shoals, or schools, of herring have almost disappeared, especially in the waters near the Shetland Islands. Long recognized as the leaders in harvesting herring, the Dutch have exploited these herring fisheries since the sixteenth century. Over time, more fishermen headed to the North Sea to gather herring. As a result, overfishing occurred and almost destroyed the shoals of herring several times.

Below: **Gulls whirl around a newly arrived fishing boat near Stornoway on Lewis Island.**

Above: **These boxes of freshly netted herring will be transported to and sold at markets.**

After one such period of overfishing in the 1870s, the fish populations revived. Yet when overfishing reoccurred, the fisheries shrank in size, forcing fishermen to sail elsewhere. Again, the fish returned and so did overharvesting. This cycle has repeated itself several times, and, since the 1960s, the world's demand for fish has increased so much that Scotland's herring have almost completely vanished.

Efforts to manage the fisheries, encourage the herring's repopulation, and limit overharvesting have been well meaning but unsuccessful in preventing the devastation of the shoals. Restrictions have been placed on catching specific breeds of fish, but, since these fish swim in areas where other breeds with less strict limitations swim, they are usually caught together. Fishermen toss the unwanted fish back into the water, where they often die. Some fishermen may sell the restricted species illegally.

Some fisheries have been closed so that the fish can freely reproduce and rebuild their species. These fisheries, however, will reopen eventually, and, unless the fishermen control how much they catch, the cycle will begin once again. Scientists have set a target goal of 800,000 tons (725,800 metric tonnes) of herring as adequate before fishing can be resumed. Technically known as the Minimum Biologically Acceptable Level, this amount is considered the minimum for the survival of the species. If the shoals of herring cannot recover, the world will lose a valuable food item.

ADVANCEMENTS IN FISHING EQUIPMENT

Technological improvements, particularly the development of steam and diesel engines, have made fishing easier and more efficient, especially by trawling. Sonar and other electronic systems have helped fishermen target where fish are swimming so they can direct their efforts to those locations. The production of certain items, such as fish oil, has also increased the rate of North Sea fishing.

Robert Louis Stevenson

Above: **Robert Louis Stevenson poses in Samoa in about 1890. Stevenson not only wrote fiction but was also a travel writer, essayist, and poet.**

Robert Louis Stevenson is known around the world for his dramatic tales of pirates and exotic places, his stories of good against evil, and his views about Scotland.

Born in Edinburgh in 1850, Robert Louis Stevenson studied law at the University of Edinburgh but decided to fulfill his childhood ambition and become a full-time writer. He suffered from tuberculosis and often traveled overseas to warmer climates to try and ease his illness. His early works describe his travels. *An Inland Voyage* was published in 1878 and told of his canoe trip through Belgium to France. The next year, he wrote *Travels with a Donkey in the Cévennes*, which described another trip in France.

In 1879, Stevenson traveled to California. The following year, he married Fanny Osbourne, an American divorcée whom he had met in 1876. They honeymooned in northern California, near an abandoned silver mine. That setting became the plot for Stevenson's *The Silverado Squatters*, written in 1883.

The couple and Fanny's son moved back to Scotland in 1881. Stevenson began writing furiously and produced *Treasure Island* (1883), one of his most famous novels. Many of his friends and associates inspired characters in his stories — Long John Silver, the peg-legged pirate in *Treasure Island*, was probably modeled after Robert's friend, W. E. Henley, who had an amputated leg.

In 1886, Stevenson wrote two books that rank among his greatest, *Kidnapped* and *The Strange Case of Dr. Jekyll and Mr. Hyde*. In 1887, Stevenson and his family returned to the United States. They sailed to New York, where he stayed for several months, enjoying fame while still writing. The following year, the family hired a yacht in San Francisco and sailed to Samoa. Samoa's climate proved to be the medicine Stevenson needed to improve his poor health, and the family moved there permanently.

Samoa provided new inspiration for the writer, who now set his stories in the Pacific Islands. His later works include *The Beach at Falesá* (1892), *The Ebb-Tide* (1894), and *In the South Seas* (1896). Robert Louis Stevenson died at the age of forty-four on December 3, 1894. His adventure novels and fantasy stories remain everpopular due to their exciting subject matter.

Opposite: **This scene from *The Strange Case of Dr. Jekyll and Mr. Hyde* shows the transformation of Dr. Henry Jekyll into Mr. Edward Hyde. Readers loved Stevenson's books, and critics admired the works for their style and presentation of moral conflicts.**

KIDNAPPED

The novel *Kidnapped*, written in 1886, deals with eighteenth-century Scottish history and evokes Stevenson's love of the Scottish landscape, history, and local atmosphere.

The Wars of Independence

Following the deaths of Alexander III in 1286 and of his granddaughter Margaret, the "Maid of Norway," four years later, the English king, Edward I (r. 1272–1307), eager to extend his rule over Scotland, appointed John Balliol as king of Scotland in 1292. Balliol rebelled against Edward I when he demanded military aid from Scotland in his war against France. Defeated by Edward I at Dunbar in April 1296, Balliol surrendered his Scottish throne to the English king. The Scots then found themselves at Edward's mercy, and the Wars of Independence erupted, as Scotland fought to remain free from the rule of the English king.

The two most famous names associated with the Wars of Independence are Sir William Wallace (c. 1270–1305) and Robert Bruce (1274–1329). Wallace led a fast-spreading movement of national resistance against English rule over Scotland. In September 1297, Wallace and his men defeated the English at Stirling Bridge but were defeated by Edward I's army at the Battle

THE STONE OF SCONE

Following the defeat of John Balliol at Dunbar in 1296, Edward I removed the coronation stone of Scone and placed it under the Coronation Chair at Westminster Abbey. The stone had been brought to Scotland by Celtic Scots and was taken to a monastery in Scone in about 840. Encased in the seat of a royal coronation chair, the stone became the ancient symbol of Scottish royalty.

Left: William Wallace was knighted and proclaimed guardian of Scotland in December 1297, following his victory at Stirling Bridge. His military reputation, however, was ruined at the Battle of Falkirk in 1298.

Opposite: Although largely outnumbered at the Battle of Bannockburn, the Scottish army overcame this disadvantage by making full use of the surrounding terrain. By confining the English army to a small marshbordered area, the Scottish prevented the enemy from moving around effectively.

of Falkirk the following year. Although Wallace was arrested and executed in London in 1305, the spirit of his revolt did not die with him.

Robert Bruce continued the fight for Scottish independence. Bruce was of noble blood and had direct ties to the monarchy. In March 1306, Bruce was crowned Robert I, king of Scotland, after killing his chief rival, John "the Red" Comyn.

Although Edward I died in 1307 and his son, Edward II (r. 1307–1327), was uninterested in warfare, the English persisted in their attempts to control Scotland. By 1314, Robert I had driven out the English garrisons from all their Scottish strongholds, except Stirling Castle. One of the most momentous battles in Scottish history took place near the castle at Bannockburn on June 23 and 24, 1314. Despite being outnumbered at least three to one, the Scottish army killed an estimated 10,000 English soldiers and claimed a great victory.

In 1320, Robert I proclaimed Scotland's independence with the signing of the Declaration of Arbroath. After the deposition of Edward II in 1327, the regency government of King Edward III (r. 1327–1377) signed the Treaty of Northampton in 1328, which officially recognized Robert I as king of an independent Scotland. Robert I died in 1329, leaving behind a free homeland.

A SPIDER'S WEB

When Robert Bruce became King of Scotland, he continued to fight for an independent Scotland. On his part, King Edward I of England made every effort to suppress the movement that he treated as a rebellion. Edward I defeated Robert I twice in 1306. Robert I's wife and many of his supporters were captured, and three of his brothers were executed. Consequently, Robert I went into hiding. While in hiding, he found inspiration from a spider. Watching the tiny spider weave its web until it was complete encouraged Robert I to continue his fight to free Scotland from English rule.

74

RELATIONS WITH NORTH AMERICA

Relations between Scotland and North America have been strong for centuries. North America is home to hundreds of thousands of people who claim Scottish or Scotch-Irish ancestry. These people have made major contributions to the political, social, and economic developments that have shaped both the United States and Canada.

Today, North Americans of Scottish descent take great interest in their family ties with Scotland. Many travel to Scotland to discover their roots, while others join organizations or societies associated with ancestral clans. North American Scots take pride in their Scottish ancestry, which is celebrated at Highland Games, at clan gatherings, and on Tartan Day. North American businesses have also established bases in Scotland because the country is a main center for oil, electronics, and biotechnology.

Opposite: **The ship *Hector* was launched in Pictou, Nova Scotia, Canada, in September 2000. The ship took ten years to build and is a replica of the original *Hector* that transported two hundred Scottish immigrants to Nova Scotia in 1773. The *Hector*'s maiden voyage was the first of many that brought Highland Scots to the New World.**

Below: **Bus tours are a popular way of seeing the sights and sounds of Edinburgh.**

Historical Links between Scotland and the United States

Turmoil and poverty in Scotland forced many Scots to leave their homeland and travel to the British North American colonies in the seventeenth century. Emigration was so common in Scotland that Scots even had a line dance called "America."

The first wave of Scottish immigrants were prisoners deported to the colonies by Oliver Cromwell (1599–1658) after the English Civil Wars of 1642 to 1651. More Scots followed after the failed Jacobite risings of 1715 and 1745. Many of these immigrants brought their Presbyterian religion with them. Today, the Presbyterian Church is one of the largest Protestant denominations in the United States, with over 3 million members.

North Carolina was an especially popular destination for Scottish immigrants in the early eighteenth century. These immigrants organized and developed markets for tobacco, which became the most important export of the colonies. Glasgow acted as the center for Europe's tobacco trade, Scotland's first major business, and the city grew rapidly.

Many Scots remained completely loyal to the British king and emotionally attached to Scotland. When the Americans revolted against British rule, Scots throughout the country formed armies, such as the Royal Highland Emigrants Regiment, and fought for Britain. When Britain lost the United States war of independence (1775–1783), thousands of Scots moved north to Canada. Other Scots, however, fought on the side of freedom.

Scots have played a part in the political history of the United States. Most notably, half the signers of the Declaration of Independence (1776) were Scots or of Scottish descent.

Besides participating in government, Scottish-Americans played a major role in establishing universities and colleges in the United States, including the College of William and Mary in Virginia.

Scottish medical establishments were well known by the seventeenth century, and a steady stream of Scottish medical doctors emigrated to the colonies. These doctors brought with them the idea that not only the body but also the mind had to be healed.

The average Scottish immigrant family worked hard to see the United States become a success. Men worked as farmers, blacksmiths, ranchers, lumberjacks, or factory employees. Their

Above: **Andrew Carnegie (1835–1919) was a Scottish-born American who became a leading steel industrialist in the late nineteenth century. He also built and equipped thousands of public libraries in the United States, set up trusts and foundations, and provided large funds for universities.**

SCOTTISH-AMERICAN GOVERNMENT OFFICIALS

Scots and their descendants have played an important role in U.S. politics. Some became presidents, including James Monroe, James Buchanan, James K. Polk, Ulysses S. Grant, Woodrow Wilson, Theodore Roosevelt, and Lyndon B. Johnson. Thirty-five Supreme Court Justices have been Scots, and many state governors have also had Scottish ancestry.

wives usually remained at home, taking care of the children and acting as nurses and teachers whenever possible.

The influence of Scotland on the United States is symbolized by place names around the country. Eight Edinburghs, eight Aberdeens, seven Glasgows, and eight places named Scotland can be found, while clans such as Cameron, Campbell, Crawford, and Douglas also gave their names to towns and counties. One area of New York where Scots settled is named Caledonian County, after the original name for Scotland.

Left: **Passengers seeking a new life in the United States disembark at New York harbor in the mid-eighteenth century, after a long journey from the Scottish Highlands.**

Historical Ties between Scotland and Canada

For centuries, Scotland has considered Canada to be an extension of itself overseas. Emigration began in the 1600s when thousands of people left Scotland and traveled to the land that eventually became known as Canada to escape religious intolerance, poverty, and starvation. They came from both the Highlands and Lowland Scotland. By the 1960s, Scottish-Canadians were the third largest ethnic group in Canada, after the English and French, a statistic that reflects their ongoing importance and influence.

Scottish immigrants settled in many parts of eastern Canada. In 1758, an army led by the Scottish Lord Rollo captured Prince Edward Island from the French, and many Scots settled on the island. In 1761, a regiment of Highland soldiers occupied Fort Frederick in New Brunswick, another Canadian province on the Atlantic coast, and soon Scots arrived from Scotland to settle the land and establish trading posts. By 1843, New Brunswick was home to well over 30,000 Scots, including thousands who had fled there from the United States after the American Revolution.

Ontario, one of Canada's most populated provinces and home to the Canadian government, was also a popular destination for Scots fleeing the United States. Bruce, Lanark, Perth, and Zora were names of settlements occupied by Scottish immigrants. Their descendants still live in those areas.

With so many Scots living in Canada, it was inevitable that some became leaders in Canada's government, economy, and society. Many prime ministers were of Scottish birth or extraction, including Sir John Alexander MacDonald, Canada's first prime minister, and Alexander Mackenzie. MacDonald was also reelected for a second term in 1878. In the twentieth century, William L. Mackenzie King led Canada through World War II and was the nation's prime minister three times, from 1921 to 1926, 1926 to 1930, and 1935 to 1948.

The majority of Canada's leading universities were established by Scots. McGill University, in Montréal, was founded in 1821 with money donated in the will of James McGill, who had emigrated from Glasgow. Another educational institution with Scottish origins is Queens, the Presbyterian University of Canada, located in Kingston, a city sometimes known as "the Aberdeen of Canada."

Above: **The first British governor of Québec was a Scot named General James Murray (1721–1794). General Murray was governor from 1760 to 1768.**

THE KING'S FIRST AMERICAN REGIMENT

Founded in New England in 1776, "The King's First American Regiment" was one of Canada's most famous regiments. The regiment consisted mainly of Scottish Highlanders who fought wearing their traditional kilts and to the sound of bagpipes. The regiment distinguished itself when it defeated General George Washington's Continental Army at the Battle of the Brandywine in 1777 during the American Revolution. When the regiment disbanded after the war, most of the soldiers settled in New Brunswick.

Nova Scotia

Nova Scotia, or New Scotland, is the Canadian province most closely linked to Scotland. Scotsman Sir William Alexander Stirling (c. 1576–1640) founded and colonized Nova Scotia in the 1620s. Throughout the 1760s and 1770s, both people from Scotland and Scots living in the United States emigrated to Nova Scotia. Following the Highland Clearances in Scotland, many Highland Scots were encouraged to head to Cape Breton to establish new settlements.

Nova Scotia's Gaelic College

Today, Nova Scotia is home to Gaelic College, the only institution of its kind in North America. Founded in 1938, the college offers programs in traditional Scottish disciplines, including Gaelic language and Celtic culture.

Below: **Inhabitants of the Outer Hebrides, ready for emigration to Canada, walk toward the SS *Marloch*, a Canadian Pacific ocean liner, moored at the pier in South Uist in early 1924.**

Historical Relations between the Scotch-Irish and North America

Between 1783 and 1812, about 100,000 Scotch-Irish emigrated to North America. Scotch-Irish are people of Scottish ancestry who settled in Northern Ireland. From 1815 to 1845, when emigration was at its peak, over 500,000 Scotch-Irish sailed to the New World. First settling in New England, New York, and Pennsylvania, the Scotch-Irish also moved south into Virginia and the Carolinas. A large number moved from New Hampshire in the United States to Truro, Nova Scotia, in 1761. After the defeat of the British in the American Revolution, many Scotch-Irish headed north to Canada. In the late 1780s, Scotch-Irish also headed to Prince Edward Island, answering a call from the government to settle there.

Wherever they settled in North America, the Scotch-Irish, like other Scottish immigrants, played a major part in the organization of overseas trade, provided communities and states with governors and clergymen, and established colleges and schools. They introduced and encouraged the practice of Presbyterianism and were leaders in politics, successful entrepreneurs, and inventors, such as Samuel Morse.

Left: Scotch-Irish Samuel Morse (1791–1872) invented the electrical telegraph between 1832 and 1835. This invention allowed encoded information to be transmitted by signal across a distance. By 1838, he had also developed the Morse Code, a system that represents letters of the alphabet, punctuation marks, and numerals by an arrangement of dots, dashes, and spaces.

Left: **Canadian Prime Minister Jean Chretien greets members of Canada's junior rugby team in Edinburgh on October 24, 1997. Jean Chretien was in Edinburgh to attend the Commonwealth Heads of Government Meeting along with representatives or heads of state from fifty other countries. During the meeting, participating countries discussed commercial and economic issues.**

Current Relations with Scotland

Despite the new political climate in Scotland after the recent reestablishment of the Scottish Parliament, relations between Scotland and North America remain strong. The nations have similar views regarding democracy, trade, human rights, terrorism, and the environment.

In April 2000, Henry McLeish, then minister for Enterprise and Lifelong Learning, went to the United States for a three-day visit. During the trip, he focused on promoting trade and tourism and expanding university and investment links that support thousands of jobs in Scotland.

The United States and Canada are vital trading partners, and the United States currently accounts for 11 percent of Scotland's exports. To nurture and develop these trading ties between Scotland and North America, business organizations have been set up to create a positive environment for transatlantic trade and investment. The Scottish North American Business Council (SNABC) was launched in December 1999 by Philip Lader, the U.S. ambassador to the United Kingdom. Officially affiliated with The British-American Business Council (BABC), SNABC currently has sixty members.

SILICON GLEN

As Scotland's economy has moved toward high-technology industries, the country now has its own version of Silicon Valley, the high-tech electronics and computer area of northern California. Scotland's version is known as Silicon Glen. Besides oil companies with headquarters in Aberdeen, other U.S. companies operating in Scotland include Ford, Polaroid, Motorola, IBM, Cisco Systems, Roche, Monsanto, Honeywell, Compaq, Oracle, Levi-Strauss, Packard Bell, Playtex, Hewlett-Packard, and Raytheon.

Scots in North America

Over two hundred thousand organizations in North America represent Scottish heritage, history, tradition, and culture. These clubs and societies celebrate Scottish ancestry. The most notable of these groups are the more than three hundred St. Andrew's Societies, Caledonian Clubs, and clan societies. Scottish-Americans and Scottish-Canadians join together to participate in festivities and take pride in their Scottish background.

Almost every week, in some part of North America, a special event takes place honoring Scottish heritage, from Highland Games and clan gatherings to monthly meetings, lectures, concerts, annual Robert Burns evenings, and St. Andrew's Day festivities. Mods also take place throughout North America, enabling people to enjoy Gaelic music, poetry, and plays. The American Scottish Foundation in New York City is a national organization whose aim is to create social and business bonds between Scotland and the United States. The organization primarily deals with Scottish-Americans wishing to learn more about their ancestry. Likewise, the United Scottish Cultural Center in Vancouver is a meeting place for anyone interested in Scottish culture.

TARTAN DAY

In 1991, the Ontario Legislature proclaimed April 6 as Tartan Day. Six years later, the U.S. Senate designated April 6 as National Tartan Day. Tartan Day recognizes the significant contributions of immigrant Scots to North America and also celebrates the traditions of Scottish culture. Today, all of North America, except for Newfoundland and Québec, celebrates Tartan Day. Special tartans have even been designed for North Americans. The tartan called "America" is designed for citizens of the United States, while the "Canadian Centennial Tartan" is the national tartan for Canadians.

Left: A policewoman gets a private Highland dance lesson from a young girl dressed in traditional Scottish attire during the Glengarry Highland Games held in Maxville, Ontario.

North Americans in Scotland

North Americans travel to Scotland for numerous reasons, including business and education. Setting up businesses in Scotland is attractive to North American companies, since Scotland has become a major center for electronics and biotechnology.

Many North Americans have become increasingly curious about their Scottish connections and travel to Scotland to explore their roots. They also head to Scotland to participate in and watch major Scottish festivals, such as Highland gatherings and the Edinburgh Military Tattoo.

North Americans have also contributed to conservation projects that preserve some of Scotland's historical sites. One such project was the restoration of Menstrie Castle near Stirling. Fearing the demolition of the castle, the birthplace of Sir William Alexander Stirling, many Nova Scotians raised funds for its restoration. The Nova Scotia Commemoration Room inside the renovated castle honors the relationship between Canada and Scotland.

During the Cold War, when the United States and the Soviet Union were political enemies, the U.S. military established bases in Scotland to protect Europe and the United States from sudden attack. One such base was Holy Loch, near Dunoon, which was transformed into a repair facility for U.S. submarines from 1960 to 1992. Today, North American military personnel are still present in Scotland but on a much smaller scale.

Above: **The U.S. relay team poses for a photograph after winning the 4 x 100-meter relay at the Norwich Union Challenge match between U.S. and British athletes at the Scotstoun Stadium in Glasgow in July 2000. The annual event attracts some of the biggest names in U.S. and British track and field. The twenty events featured include sprints, hurdles, field events, and relays.**

Hollywood Legends

Clark Gable (1901–1960) and James Stewart (1908–1997), two of Hollywood's greatest actors, were of Scottish ancestry. Known as the "king of Hollywood," Clark Gable is probably best known for his portrayal of Rhett Butler in *Gone with the Wind*, while James Stewart starred in such classics as *The Philadelphia Story*, *The Man Who Knew Too Much*, and *Vertigo*. Both actors were highly respected stars of the silver screen.

Many of Scotland's talented actors continue to perform in Hollywood blockbusters. Sir Sean Connery is perhaps best known for his on-screen portrayal of Ian Fleming's secret agent James Bond. A new generation of actors has recently emerged from Scotland, most notably Ewan McGregor, who starred as Obi-Wan Kenobi in George Lucas's Star Wars movie *Episode 1: The Phantom Menace*; Robert Carlyle, whose films include *Angela's Ashes* and *The Beach*; and John Hannah, who starred in *Sliding Doors* and *The Mummy*.

THE DUKE

Born Marion Michael Morrison in 1907, American John Wayne, also known as the Duke, had Scotch-Irish ancestry. Wayne was one of the greatest box-office stars in movie history. He starred in more than 250 movies and won an Academy Award for best actor for his portrayal of Rooster Cogburn in *True Grit*.

Below: Ewan McGregor (*left*) and Sean Connery (*right*) are two of Scotland's most popular actors.

Sports

Scottish immigrants brought popular Scottish sports, such as golf and curling, to North America. Golf was played in North America by the seventeenth century, but it did not develop as an organized sport until 1888 when St. Andrews Golf Club in Yonkers, New York, was established by John Reid and Robert Lockhart, both Scots. Today, more than 23 million people in the United States alone play golf.

Curling has also found a place in North American sports. In the United States, the Grand National Curling Club of America was formed in 1867. In 1957, the first U.S. championship was held in Chicago, and the United States Curling Association was organized in 1958. A Canadian branch of the Royal Caledonian Curling Club was founded in 1852, and the Royal Montreal Curling Club has existed since 1907. The Canadian championship began in 1927 and became the world's biggest curling event. Canada proved its domination in the sport when it won double gold at the 2000 Ford World Curling Championship held at Braehead Arena in Glasgow, Scotland.

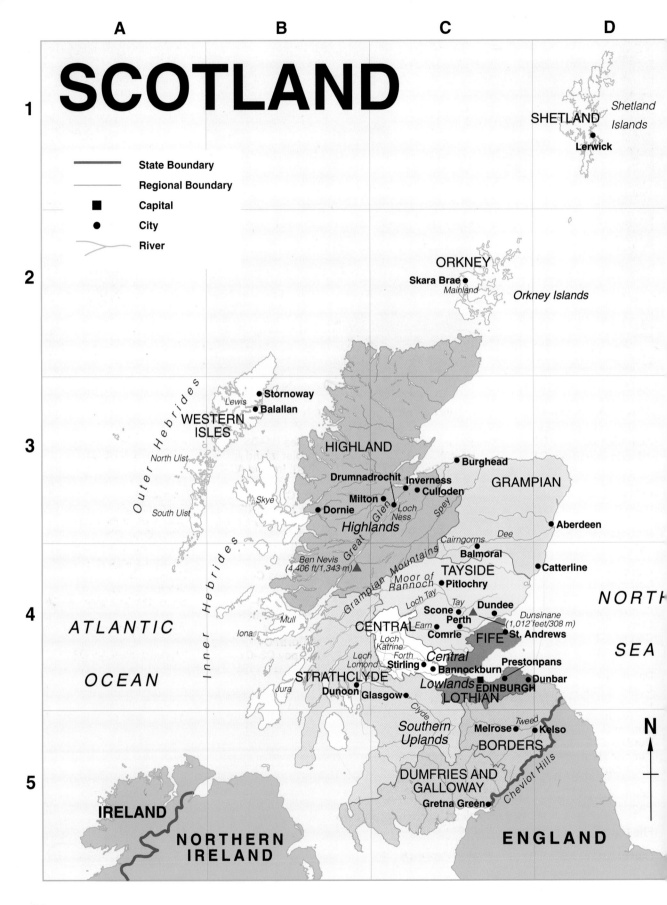

SCOTLAND

SHETLAND

*Shetland
Islands*

● Lerwick

State Boundary
Regional Boundary
■ Capital
● City
River

ORKNEY

Skara Brae ●
Mainland

Orkney Islands

● Stornoway
● Balallan

Lewis

WESTERN
ISLES

HIGHLAND

● Burghead

North Uist

Drumnadrochit
● Inverness
● Culloden

GRAMPIAN

● Milton

Skye

Loch
Ness

● Dornie

Highlands

South Uist

Outer Hebrides

Spey

Great
Glen

Cairngorms

Dee

● Aberdeen

● Balmoral

Ben Nevis
(4,406 ft/1,343 m) ▲

Grampian Mountains

● Catterline

TAYSIDE

Inner Hebrides

*Moor of
Rannoch*

● Pitlochry

Mull

Loch Tay

Tay

● Dundee

Iona

Scone ●
● Perth

▲ Dunsinane
(1,012 feet/308 m)

ATLANTIC

CENTRAL

Earn

Comrie ●

● St. Andrews

FIFE

Loch
Katrine

Loch
Lomond

Forth

Central

Prestonpans ●

● Stirling
● Bannockburn

OCEAN

Jura

STRATHCLYDE

Lowlands

EDINBURGH ■

● Dunbar

● Dunoon

● Glasgow

LOTHIAN

NORTH

SEA

Clyde

*Southern
Uplands*

Tweed

● Melrose

● Kelso

BORDERS

N
↑

DUMFRIES AND
GALLOWAY

Cheviot Hills

IRELAND

● Gretna Green

ENGLAND

NORTHERN
IRELAND

Above: Skiers head for the lodge after a long day of skiing in the Cairngorms.

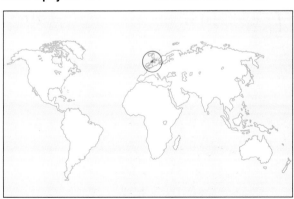

SCOTLAND

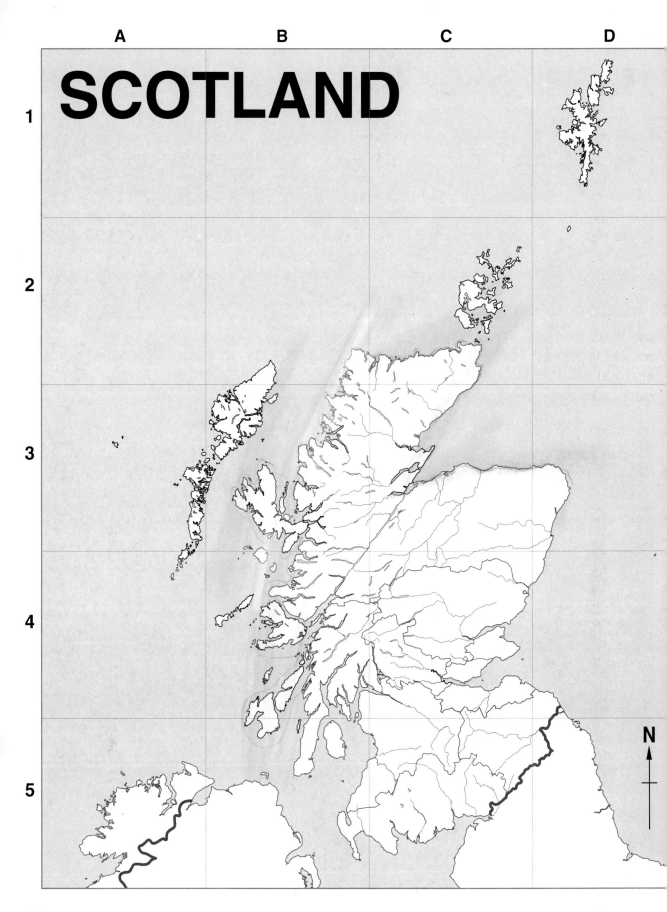

How Is Your Geography?

Learning to identify the main geographical areas and points of a country can be challenging. Although it may seem difficult at first to memorize the locations and spellings of major cities or the names of mountain ranges, rivers, deserts, lakes, and other prominent physical features, the end result of this effort can be very rewarding. Places you previously did not know existed will suddenly come to life when referred to in world news, whether in newspapers, television reports, or other books and reference sources. This knowledge will make you feel a bit closer to the rest of the world, with its fascinating variety of cultures and physical geography.

Used in a classroom setting, the instructor can make duplicates of this map using a copy machine. (PLEASE DO NOT WRITE IN THIS BOOK!) Students can then fill in any requested information on their individual map copies. Used one-on-one, the student can also make copies of the map on a copy machine and use them as a study tool. The student can practice identifying place names and geographical features on his or her own.

Above: **Adventurous Scots enjoy the craggy beauty of the Cairngorms.**

Scotland at a Glance

Official Name	Scotland (part of United Kingdom of Great Britain and Northern Ireland)
Capital	Edinburgh
Official Language	English
National Languages	Gaelic, Scots
Population	5.1 million (2001 estimate)
Land Area	30,418 square miles (78,783 square km)
Regions	Borders, Central, Dumfries and Galloway, Fife, Grampian, Highland, Lothian, Strathclyde, Tayside
Island Areas	Orkney, Shetland, Western Isles
Highest Point	Ben Nevis 4,406 feet (1,343 m)
Major Rivers	Clyde, Tay
Major Lakes	Loch Katrine, Loch Lomond, Loch Ness, Loch Tay
Major Cities	Aberdeen, Edinburgh, Glasgow
Main Religions	Church of Scotland (Presbyterianism denomination), Roman Catholicism
Major Industries	Electronics, manufacturing, North Sea oil and gas, textiles, whiskey production
Major Festivals	Edinburgh Military Tattoo (August)
	Halloween (October 31)
	Saint Andrew's Day (November 30)
	Hogmanay (December 31)
Famous Scots	Robert the Bruce, Robert Burns, Sir William Wallace
Currency	Pound Sterling (£0.70 = U.S. $1 in 2000)

Opposite: **The gardens and fountain surrounding Edinburgh Castle offer breathtaking views on a beautiful summer day.**

Glossary

French Vocabulary

flambeaux (flam-BOH): beautiful flames; the term used to describe a fire festival celebrated every New Year in Comrie.

Gaelic Vocabulary

ceilidh (KAY-lee): a social gathering that involves dancing, drinking, singing, and storytelling; a type of music directly associated with dancing.

feileadh-beg (EH-leh-beg): little kilt.

feileadh-mór (EH-leh-mor): great plaid.

Gaelic (GAY-lik): a Celtic language, spoken in Ireland and Scotland.

Gillie Callum (GEE-leh HAL-um): sword dance; a traditional Highland dance.

guizers (GUY-zers): a parade of Vikings that participates in Up-Helly-Aa.

Lallans (LAH-lanz): Scots, the language spoken in southern Scotland.

Oidche Challainn (EYE-shee-ah KHAH-lin): evening of the oatcake; the term used to describe New Year.

Seann Truibhas (SHAWN trews): Old Trousers; a traditional Highland dance.

sínteag (SHEEN-tee-ak): to skip or leap.

uisge beatha (OOSH-kee-ah BEH-er): the water of life; the term used to describe whiskey.

Scots Vocabulary

feides (fides): feud.

English Vocabulary

advocate: a person who supports a particular cause.

animosities: strong feelings of dislike.

art nouveau: a design style of the late nineteenth and early twentieth centuries characterized by wavy lines and leaflike forms.

barrow: a hill.

black bun: a rich fruitcake, made with raisins, currants, orange and lemon peel, chopped almonds, and brown sugar.

brochs: round, towerlike structures open in the middle, dating from the first century A.D.

civil law: a system of law derived from ancient Rome that deals with people's private matters, as opposed to criminal, political, or military matters.

common law: a system of law originating in England that is based on court decisions and on custom rather than on written laws.

crannogs: artificial, fortified islands constructed in a lake or marsh.

crofts: small farms that are settled and worked by tenants.

culture dish: a container used to grow microorganisms or tissues.

de facto: already existing, although not legally recognized.

defied: challenged the power of a person, organization, or government.

devolution: the transfer of power or authority to a local government from a central government.

dirk: a long dagger with a straight blade.

eerie: strange; frightening.

epitomize: to serve as an ideal example of.

ethnic cleansing: the elimination of an unwanted ethnic group from society.

feudalism: the political, military, and social system in the Middle Ages, having as its basis the relation between lord and subject. All land is owned by the lord but worked by the subject in exchange for a rent payment and /or military service.

forfeited: lost the right to.

fortifications: buildings constructed to defend or strengthen a position.

garrisons: groups of troops stationed in a fortified place.

Gothic: a style of architecture characterized by tall pillars, high curved ceilings, and pointed arches.

hearty: substantial, abundant, or nourishing.

hill forts: fortified sites, often at the top of a hill, dating back to the Iron Ages.

hoax: something intended to deceive.

hue and cry: a loud outcry once used in the pursuit of criminals.

hydrofoil: a boat that has metal plates or fins fitted to lift the hull clear of the water as a certain speed is attained.

instigated: urged, provoked, or incited into some course of action.

intermediary: someone who acts as a mediator, or go-between, between persons or parties.

loch: a lake.

logarithms: exponents; numbers used to represent the repeated multiplications of a given number.

neoclassical: a style of architecture that is influenced by Roman and Greek architecture.

Neolithic: characteristic of the latest phase of the Stone Age, which began in about 9000–8000 B.C.

peat: an organic material found in marshy or damp regions, composed of partially decayed vegetable matter. Peat is cut, dried, and used as fuel.

plesiosaur: any extinct marine reptile of the Jurassic suborder Plesiosauria, having a thick body and paddlelike limbs.

posses: groups of people summoned for the purpose of making a search.

referendum: the practice of submitting to popular vote a measure that has been proposed by a legislative body.

Reformation: a religious movement that resulted in the formation of new Protestant religions throughout Europe during the sixteenth century.

Roman: in architecture, a style of architecture characterized by semicircular arches and domes.

sept: a branch of a family or clan.

socialism: a system in which the production and distribution of goods are owned and controlled collectively or by the government.

spores: cells produced by bacteria and fungi that develop into new forms of bacteria.

sporran: a pouch made of skin with the hair or fur still attached.

squat: short and thick.

strife: bitter conflict, struggle, or clash.

tempo: the speed at which a piece of music is played.

tiddledywinks: a game in which players make small plastic disks jump from a flat surface into a cup by pressing on their edges.

More Books to Read

Fairy Tales from Scotland. Oxford Story Collections series. Barbara Ker Wilson (Oxford University Press)

The Far Side of the Loch. Little House series. Melissa Wiley (HarperTrophy)

Kidnapped. Robert Louis Stevenson (Penguin USA)

Letters Home from Scotland. Letters Home From series. Marcia S. Gresko (Blackbirch Marketing)

Queen's Own Fool: A Novel of Mary, Queen of Scots. Jane Yolen (Philomel Books)

Scotland. Origins series. Mike Hirst (Franklin Watts)

Scotland: Togs and Clogs. Cultures of the World series. Patricia Levy (Benchmark Books)

Scottish Clans and Tartans. Looking into the Past series. Dwayne E. Pickels (Chelsea House Publishing)

Stone Age Farmers Beside the Sea: Scotland's Prehistoric Village of Skara Brae. Caroline Arnold (Clarion Books)

Videos

Castles of Scotland. (Acorn Media)

Scotland . . . Beauty and Majesty. (BFS Entertainment & Multimedia)

Scotland the Brave. (Acorn Media)

William Wallace. (Kultur Video)

Web Sites

www.infoplease.kids.lycos.com/ce6/world/A0844104.htm

www.myspace.co.uk/nessie/nessie/search.html

www.stonepages.com/scotland/scotland.html

www.tartans.com

Due to the dynamic nature of the Internet, some web sites stay current longer than others. To find additional web sites, use a reliable search engine with one or more of the following keywords to help you locate information about Scotland. Keywords: *bagpipes, Robert Burns, curling, Edinburgh, Glasgow, haggis, Highland Games, Scottish clans, shinty.*

Index